ALCOHOL AND DRUG ABUSE

PREVENTING UNDERAGE DRINKING

WHAT WORKS?

ALCOHOL AND DRUG ABUSE

Additional books in this series can be found on Nova's website under the Series tab.

Additional e-books in this series can be found on Nova's website under the eBooks tab.

CHILDREN'S ISSUES, LAWS AND PROGRAMS

Additional books in this series can be found on Nova's website under the Series tab.

Additional e-books in this series can be found on Nova's website under the eBooks tab.

ALCOHOL AND DRUG ABUSE

PREVENTING UNDERAGE DRINKING

WHAT WORKS?

MICHAEL L. LEGRAND
EDITOR

nova
New York

Library of Congress Cataloging-in-Publication Data

ISBN: 978-1-53613-632-6

Published by Nova Science Publishers, Inc. † New York

CONTENTS

PREFACE[1]

This book was reprinted from a public document and records from the US Government. It is a collection of hearings that took place in Washington DC by the Committee on Education and the Workforce, U.S. House of Representatives on February 11th 2004.

According to Mrs. Wendy J. Hamilton, the national President of Mothers Against Drunk Driving, where she has served since 2002 (after three separate drunk driving crashes occurred within her family) – "Alcohol is the illegal drug of choice for America's youth … [it] is a major factor in the three leading causes of death of America's teens…. Teens have easy access to alcohol…[and] the consequences are staggering." This book provides statistics about the amount of teenagers who drink and the amount of deaths per year it contributes to. It also examines the Programs already in force for underage drinking, including Youth in Action, as well as provides recommendations on how to reduce the amount of young people who drink. It also includes education-oriented interventions that should be implemented to prevent underage drinking in the future.

---

[1] This is an edited, reformatted and augmented version of Committee on Education and the Workforce, Hearing before the Subcommittee on Education Reform of the Committee on Education and the Workforce, U.S. House of Representatives, One Hundred Eighth Congress, Second Session, Serial No. 108-42, dated February 11, 2004.

Chapter 1

HEARING HELD ON FEBRUARY 11, 2004

SUBCOMMITTEE ON EDUCATION REFORM

Committee on Education and the Workforce: Washington, DC

The Subcommittee met, pursuant to notice, at 11:35 a.m., in room 2175, Rayburn House Office Building, Hon. Michael N. Castle [Chairman of the Subcommittee] presiding.

Present: Representatives Castle, Osborne, Upton, Keller, Wilson, Woolsey, Davis of California, Davis of Illinois, Case, Kind, and Van Hollen.

Ex officio present: Representative Owens.

Staff present: Kevin Frank, Professional Staff Member; Catherine Meyer, Legislative Assistant; Krisann Pearce, Deputy Director of Education and Human Resources Policy; Whitney Rhoades, Professional Staff Member; Deborah L. Samantar, Committee Clerk/Intern Coordinator; Jo-Marie St. Martin, General Counsel; Liz Wheel, Legislative Assistant; Joe Novotny, Minority Legislative Assistant/Education; and Lynda Theil, Minority Legislative Associate/Education.

Chairman Castle. A quorum being present, the Subcommittee on Education Reform of the Committee on Education and the Workforce will come to order.

We are meeting today to hear testimony on "Preventing Underage Drinking: What Works?" So that we can get to our witnesses, I am going to limit the opening statements to the Chairman, the ranking minority member, and the designee from each side. Therefore, if other members have statements, they will be included in the hearing record.

With that, I ask unanimous consent for the hearing record to remain open 14 days to allow members' statements and other extraneous material referenced during the hearing to be submitted in the official hearing record.

Without objection, so ordered.

Chapter 2

STATEMENT OF MEMBERS

STATEMENT OF HON. MICHAEL N. CASTLE, CHAIRMAN, SUBCOMMITTEE ON EDUCATION REFORM, COMMITTEE ON EDUCATION AND THE WORKFORCE

Let me say, first of all, good morning to everyone here, including, of course, our witnesses. I would like to welcome all of our guests and our witnesses and our members who are here for today's Education Reform Subcommittee hearing entitled, "Preventing Underage Drinking: What Works?"

I am looking forward to hearing the witnesses' testimony pertaining to the efforts these organizations are making to help reduce and prevent underage drinking in this country. Today's hearing will focus on awareness and prevention programs that are geared toward students in elementary, middle and high school that successfully prevent and discourage youth from drinking alcohol before they are of legal age.

Significant gains have been made in reducing underage drinking since the 1970's and the 1980's. I applaud the various local, state and Federal Governmental organizations, the public health community groups, and the members of industry who have contributed to this reduction. I know that in my home state of Delaware there are numerous efforts at all levels of government.

However, this issue remains a real problem with very real and devastating consequences. Despite the progress that has been made, the 2002 National Survey on Drug Use and Health administered by the Substance Abuse and Mental Health Administration found that 10.7 million young people, ages 12 to 20, reported drinking alcohol within a 30-day period. About three in ten high school seniors reported binge drinking, binge drinkers defined as those having five or more drinks on the same occasion at least once in the past 30 days.

The study also reported that 95 percent of 12th graders perceived alcohol as readily available to them.

It is my hope that we can better learn what constitutes an effective awareness and prevention program so that these best practices can be shared with schools and communities throughout the country. Programs based on research and whose effectiveness has been evaluated are invaluable.

I would like to thank my colleague from Nebraska, Mr. Osborne, for his interest in this issue and for his dedication to reducing and preventing underage drinking. It was his interest and tenacity that was the impetus for this hearing.

I now yield to the distinguished ranking minority member of the Subcommittee, Mrs. Woolsey, for purposes of making an opening statement.

[The prepared statement of Mr. Castle follows:]

Statement of Hon. Michael N. Castle, Chairman, Subcommittee on Education Reform, Committee on Education and the Workforce

Good Morning. I would like to welcome our guests, witnesses, and members to today's Education Reform Subcommittee hearing entitled, "Preventing Underage Drinking: What Works?"

I am looking forward to hearing the witness' testimony pertaining to the efforts these organizations are making to help reduce and prevent underage drinking in this country. Today's hearing will focus on awareness and prevention programs that are geared toward students in elementary, middle, and high school that successfully prevent and discourage youth from drinking alcohol before they are of legal age.

Significant gains have been made in reducing underage drinking since the 1970's and 1980's. I applaud the various local, state, and federal governmental organizations, the public health community groups, and the members of industry that have contributed to this reduction. I know that in my home state of Delaware there are numerous efforts, at all levels of government. However, this issue remains a real problem with very real and devastating consequences. Despite the progress that has been made, the 2002 National Survey on Drug Use and Health, administered by the Substance Abuse and Mental Health Administration, found that 10.7 million young people, ages 12 to 20, reported drinking alcohol within a 30-day period. About 3 in 10 high school seniors reported binge drinking—binge drinkers defined as those having five or more drinks on the same occasion at least once in the past 30 days.

The study also reported that 95 percent of 12th graders perceive alcohol as readily available to them.

It is my hope that we can better learn what constitutes an effective awareness and prevention program so that these best practices can be shared with schools and communities throughout the country. Programs based on research and whose effectiveness has been evaluated are invaluable.

I would like to thank my colleague from Nebraska, Mr. Osborne for his interest in this issue and for his dedication to reducing and preventing underage drinking.

It was his interest and tenacity that was the impetus for this hearing.

With that, I yield to my colleague from California, Mrs. Woolsey for whatever opening statement she may have.

Statement of Hon. Lynn Woolsey, Ranking Member, Subcommittee on Education Reform, Committee on Education and the Workforce

Ms. Woolsey. Thank you very much, Mr. Chairman, and thank you for this hearing. It is very important. Underage drinking is a serious public health and safety program and it is also very, very expensive for our country.

Alcohol is a key factor in the three leading causes of death among young people in America—traffic crashes, homicides, and suicides. Alcohol kills 6.5 times as many American youth as illegal drugs combined. The economic consequences of underage drinking are also huge.

The Pacific Institute for Research and Evaluation researched the cost to society of underage drinking in a report prepared in the year 2002 and found them to be more than $58 billion per year.

Yet we have a robust Federal youth anti-drug campaign and no Federal campaign to combat underage drinking.

In fact, in his fiscal year '05 budget, President Bush has recommended eliminating funding for the one Federal school-based alcohol prevention program which is currently authorized under the Safe and Drug-Free Schools Act. This must change.

In September of 2003 the Institutes of Medicine at the National Academy of Sciences issued a report to Congress entitled, "Reducing Underage Drinking: A Collective Responsibility." The panel of public health experts who wrote this report found that not only is alcohol easy for underage youth to obtain, but also that their main source of alcohol is adults, both in social settings and in stores. The panel also found alcohol product advertising to be a strong contributing factor to underage drinking.

So when we talk about programs that work to prevent underage drinking we need to remember that along with programs that focus directly on the youth, we also need programs to educate adults about what they do to contribute to underage drinking, and we need to have better constraints on advertising and marketing alcohol to youth of those ages. In my district

I am really pleased to say that in my district an alcohol beverage distributor called Golden Gate Distributing Company has been constantly involved with local police departments and their programs to curb underage drinking.

Golden Gate Distributing has been involved—well, they are a 70-year-old distributing company, and they have been involved for years at our local high schools with their safe graduation nights and they work to make sure that we are totally involved in their programs to combat underage drinking. They would like the Federal Government to understand that not all distributors are out to get kids to drink; and we can use what they are doing as one of our examples but what we have to know—all these examples are not leading to the results we want so we have to do more. That is what I hope we will be hearing from you about.

I am pleased today that Jacqueline Hackett is here to tell her story about Students Against Destructive Decisions (SADD)—what a great way to do this—which is an outstanding national program that does focus directly on youth. SADD provides students with prevention and intervention tools, the tools they need to deal with underage drinking and other harmful behaviors, and SADD has a proven track record of success.

I look forward to hearing from you, Jackie, and I would like to greet the Honorable Susan Molinari, a past Member of Congress who still feels like she is in our halls. Thank you for coming, Susan.

[The prepared statement of Ms. Woolsey follows:]

Statement of Hon. Lynn Woolsey, Ranking Member, Subcommittee on Education Reform, Committee on Education and the Workforce

Thank you for calling this hearing, Mr. Chairman. Underage drinking is a serious public health and safety problem, as well as a very costly one.

Alcohol is a key factor in the three leading causes of death among young people in America: traffic crashes; homicides; and suicides. Alcohol kills six and half times as many American youth as all illegal drugs combined.

The economic consequences of underage drinking are also huge—the Pacific Institute for Research and Evaluation researched the costs to society of underage drinking in a report prepared in 2002 and found them to be more than $58 billion per year.

Yet, we have a robust federal youth anti-drug campaign and no federal campaign to combat underage drinking. In fact, in his fiscal year 05 budget, president bush has recommended eliminating funding for the one federal school-based alcohol prevention program, which is currently authorized under the safe and drug-free schools act.

That must change.

In September of 2003, the Institutes of Medicine at the National Academy of Sciences issued a report to congress, "Reducing Underage Drinking: A Collective Responsibility."

The panel of public health experts who wrote this report found that not only is alcohol easy for underage youth to obtain, but also that their main source of alcohol is adults, in both social settings and stores. The panel also found alcohol product advertising to be a strong contributing factor to underage drinking.

So, when we talk today about programs that work to prevent underage drinking, we need to remember that along with programs that focus directly on youth, we also need programs to educate adults about the things that we do to contribute to underage drinking and we also need better restraints on advertising and marketing alcohol to underage youth.

Having said that, I am pleased today to have Ms. Jacqueline Hackett here to tell us about SADD (Students Against Destructive Decisions), an outstanding national program that does focus directly on youth. SADD provides students with the prevention and intervention tools they need to deal with underage drinking and other harmful behaviors, and it has a proven track record of success. I look forward to hearing from Jacqueline and the rest of the panel.

Chairman Castle. Thank you, Ms. Woolsey. We appreciate your good comments.

The opening statement indicated we would have a designee on each side, and I will now turn to the distinguished gentleman from Nebraska, Mr. Osborne, for his 5 minutes.

STATEMENT OF HON. TOM OSBORNE, A REPRESENTATIVE IN CONGRESS FROM THE STATE OF NEBRASKA

Mr. Osborne. Thank you, Chairman Castle. I would like to thank you and also Chairman Boehner for allowing us to have this hearing.

The reason I was interested in this is that I spent about 36 years on a college campus, and I would say probably 70 to maybe 90 percent of the problems that I saw and I dealt with, whether it be assaults, sexual assault, accidents, and sometimes criminal behavior, have usually involved alcohol, and usually it was underage drinking.

So at the present time, more than one-fourth of Nebraska young people indicate that they first use alcohol by age 13, and I believe nationally the average age of first drink is under age 13. We are not really aiming here at 21, 20, 19-year-olds. We are really concerned about what is going on at 11 and 12 and 13 and 14 and 15.

And this is a big problem. There is an estimated 3 million teenagers in our country today that are full-blown alcoholics, and that is a huge number when you look at other types of addiction. That is by far the most.

It has already been mentioned that alcohol kills six times more young people than all other illicit drugs and I think Ms. Woolsey mentioned $58 billion as the annual cost. I have seen $53 billion, but it is certainly in the $50 billions.

We just had a meeting, Republicans did, about the budget deficit, and $53 billion would go a long ways, I mean if we could even trim that in half, because somebody is paying for that and basically it is the taxpayers that are paying for that $53 billion.

Those who use alcohol before age 15 are four times more likely to become alcohol-dependent. The thing I think that I would like to emphasize here is that there is a physiological and psychological component. When you are 12 and 13 and 14, 15, that is way different in the use of alcohol than if you are 21, 22, 23 years of age.

It has an entirely different reaction on the human body and on the brain, and these are the kids that we are dealing with.

Underage drinkers consume nearly twice as much alcohol per occasion as adults and that is a binge drink, and oftentimes what they do is they drink to get drunk. They don't drink to be sociable, they drink to get drunk.

Alcohol is the most widely used drug among America's young people, yet the Federal Government spends 25 times more on prevention of illicit drug use by young people than on prevention of underage drinking, so it is our biggest problem. And yet we spend $1/25^{th}$ of our prevention dollars on alcohol, which seems a little bit skewed as far as I am concerned.

In May of 2001 the General Accounting Office released a report, and the report provided concrete evidence that, No. 1, the Federal Government's approach to youth alcohol prevention is disjointed, and, No. 2, funding for alcohol youth prevention is woefully inadequate.

So as Ms. Woolsey mentioned, we are really concerned to see the $30 million for alcohol abuse reduction zeroed out in the '05 budget. Again, talking about the budget process, we realize there's going to be casualties, but if you can do something to reduce a $53 billion taxpayer bill by spending $30 million, it might be money well spent.

Then also, September 2003, the National Academy of Science reported and they recommended this, a national adult-oriented media campaign as the centerpiece of Federal efforts to prevent underage drinking. The problem is that so many adults actually are sometimes relieved if their child uses alcohol, because they say if they are using alcohol, they are not going to use anything else. Well, anybody who knows anything about this problem realizes that kids, once they become addicted will grab anything they can. They don't start with meth. They don't start with cocaine. They start with alcohol, sometimes with marijuana and then it goes from there. So we need to educate adults as to what is going on out there.

Secondly, the alcohol industry should strengthen its current voluntary advertising codes, refrain from marketing practices that have substantial appeal to youth and be more careful to place under ads to reduce youthful exposure.

Then, third, the need for better Federal coordination and assistance to states and local communities.

Lastly, let me just say this. I know there are representatives of the alcohol industry here and I think many of you do some great things. I know your intentions are very good but I would have to confess some skepticism in regard to some of the claims that people in alcohol industry have made.

For example, the director of product development at Anheuser-Busch, in commenting on Bacardi Silver, said this: "This beauty of this category is that it brings in new drinkers, people who really don't like the taste of beer. Industry trade reporters call these beverages teeny-bopper sweet drinks," so they appeal heavily to underage drinkers.

A recent Monitoring the Future survey indicates that 50 percent of high school seniors have consumed Alco-Pops, which taste like soda pop, which, again, appeals to youth to drink. Malibu Rum has U-Shaggy to promote its products. Shaggy won two Teen Choice awards in 2001 and recently Anheuser-Busch assigned Sergio Garcia, age 22, to a Michelob sponsorship agreement, and the Beer Institute marketing advertising code stipulates models and actors used in ads should be a minimum of 25 years old and on and on and on.

Beer advertisement providing steady exposure to talking animals, pop culture, immature humor, encourages underage drinking.

So anyway, these are some of the concerns I have and I want to thank you witnesses for being here today. I look forward to hearing your thoughts and suggestions of how we can strengthen underage drinking prevention programs and again, Mr. Chairman, appreciate your having this hearing.

Chairman Castle. Thank you, Mr. Osborne.

We will now turn to our witnesses, and we have a very distinguished panel of witnesses before us today. I will go through all the introductions and then we will go through the format, how we will proceed.

The first speaker will be the Honorable Susan Molinari, who is currently the chairman of the Century Council, a not-for-profit organization that seeks to fight drunk driving and underage drinking. She is also president and CEO of the Washington Group. Previously Congresswoman Molinari represented a congressional district in New York from 1990 to 1997, where she was elected to the Republican majority leadership. She is the chair of the Ripon Educational Fund and serves as a national spokesperson for Americans for Consumer Education and Competition, and she was a very successful Member of Congress when she was here, and we welcome her back.

All of you will have 5 minutes to speak. Former Members of Congress only get 1 minute.

[Laughter.]

Chairman Castle. So she will be a little bit limited in what she says.

And I understand that Mr. Osborne would like to introduce the next witness on our panel today, and I yield to him for that purpose.

Mr. Osborne. Well, it's my pleasure to introduce Bob Newton. I met Bob 36 years ago. He was at Cerritos Junior College in California, played a little football there, came to the University of Nebraska in 1969 and played there in 1969-70 and was an All-American player at Nebraska, went on to play with the Chicago Bears from 1971 through 1976, Seattle Seahawks from 1977 to 1982—I may have those years off a little bit, but he spent 11 years in pro football.

In 1983 he came back to University of Nebraska and eventually got a master's degree, went through some procedures he may tell you about, and eventually became a drug and alcohol counselor, worked for Lincoln Council on Alcohol and Drugs, later went to Seattle, worked as a drug counselor out there, worked with the Seahawks in a capacity as a drug and alcohol counselor, and now he works with Betty Ford as the director of business development.

And he also is a certified drug and alcohol counselor, does a lot of speaking around the country, and he knows this issue inside and out, so I am glad that he could be here today.

Chairman Castle. Thank you, Mr. Osborne, and nice to have you here, Mr. Newton.

Our next witness is Mrs. Wendy J. Hamilton. She is currently the national president of Mothers Against Drunk Driving, where she has served since 2002. She began her efforts with MADD after three separate drunk driving crashes occurred within her family, and prior to her current position, Mrs. Hamilton served MADD in several positions, including vice president of victim issues, vice president of field issues, and as public policy liaison.

Next will be Jacqueline Hackett, who has already been mentioned. Ms. Hackett is currently a senior at Souderton Area High School in Souderton, Pennsylvania, where she participates in various activities—quite a few activities, as a matter of fact. She serves on the student leadership council for Students Against Destructive Decisions. Additionally, she is a DARE role model as well as a member of the Just Say No Traveling Show.

Ms. Hackett has been recognized in Who's Who among American High School Seniors and is a member of the National Honor Roll and the National Honor Society.

Our final witness will be Mrs. Francine Katz. Mrs. Katz is the vice president of corporate communications at Anheuser-Busch Companies, Incorporated. Her duties include overseeing the departments responsible for Anheuser-Busch's alcohol awareness and education programs for both underage and adult audiences as well as the company's archives and library.

Prior to joining Anheuser-Busch Mrs. Katz practiced law for 5 years in St. Louis, where she specialized in general corporate law.

She is a member of various boards, including St. Louis University, the Mary Institute and County Day School, and the St. Louis Children's Hospital Developmental Board.

Let me just say before the witnesses begin to testify that the whole panel will testify and then we will have questions back and forth from the members up here. It is a 5-minute limit in both instances.

Let me apologize. As some of you may know, we all serve on more than one Committee and I am serving on the Financial Services Committee and Mr. Alan Greenspan is testifying there, and it is time for me to ask him questions, and try to straighten out our economy, so I am going to run over there for a while, and turn this over to Mr. Osborne as we proceed with our witnesses.

With that, we will turn to Susan Molinari.

Chapter 3

Statement of Witnesses

Statement of Hon. Susan Molinari, Chairman, the Century Council, Washington, D.C.

Ms. Molinari. Thank you very much, Chairman Castle and other members of this Committee. It is truly a pleasure for me to be here. I will be on the other side of the podium than when Congressman Boehner—Chairman Boehner and I served many years together on this Committee, and it truly is an honor to be back here.

May I say that I would not be surprised to come back here in a few short years and find Ms. Hackett sitting on the other side of this dais herself, based on the background that she has accrued for herself at such a young age.

I am delighted to be here today as a former Member of Congress, but very important to today's mission as chairman of the Century Council. The Century Council is an independent, national, not-for-profit organization with two missions—fighting drunk driving and underage drinking. It is headquartered here in Washington, D.C. and is funded by America's leading distillers. Our council's mission is to promote responsible decision making regarding drinking or not drinking of beverage alcohol and to discourage all forms of irresponsible consumption through education, communications, working with law enforcement, and in conjunction with other program partners.

Now since 1933 the distilled spirits industry has initiated and supported programs designed to fight alcohol abuse. In the testimony I have submitted I have provided you examples of those efforts in greater detail.

Today, let me talk about the Century Council, which was formed in 1991 and is funded by Allied Domecq Spirits and Wine, North America, Bacardi USA, Brown Forman, DIAGEO, Future Brands, LLC, and Pernod Ricard USA. They have invested together more than $130-140 million to support the council's efforts to develop and implement alcohol education and prevention programs.

We posted over 2000 events to launch our programs. Just launching our programs in communities across the nation, bringing them to millions of parents, kids, educators, law enforcement officials, and traffic safety professionals.

We are joined and work in conjunction with an independent advisory board of distinguished leaders in business, government, education, medicine and all other relevant disciplines to assist the counsel in development of its programs and its policies.

Now the council's education efforts start in middle school and continue on through college—programs such as the *Ready or Not* program, which is a video-based program currently being utilized in boys' and girls' clubs across the country.

The Brandon Silveria Make the Right Choice is a speaking tour by a young man who was involved in an alcohol-related crash in high school. Parents, You're Not Done Yet is a brochure that encourages parents to talk with their kids before they leave for college about the dangers of underage drinking, very much to your point, Congressman Osborne.

Cops in Shops is a cooperative effort involving local retailers such as the ones Congresswoman Woolsey talked about and law enforcement designed to deter minors from attempting to purchase alcohol illegally and adults who purchase alcohol for minors.

Our latest, Alcohol 101 Plus, is an innovative CD-ROM program aimed at helping students make safe and responsible decisions about alcohol on college campuses.

In fact, many Members of Congress have participated in, I think close to 200 now, and have shared these programs with their constituents, such as the Brandon program, which was a program that I used in my high schools when I was a Member of Congress and was my first introduction to the council's good work.

Now important progress has been made in reducing underage drinking over the past few decades. Implementation of effective programs has resulted in fewer alcohol-related deaths and injuries among youth, but clearly, and we are grateful for your presence here today because so much more needs to be done.

The 2003 Monitoring the Future study revealed that alcohol consumption was relatively unchanged in 2003, unfortunately, after declining in 2002. Despite the lack of significant decrease in consumption, high school seniors who reported daily drinking in the past months declined 32 percent proportionately, but despite this notable progress, as you stated very correctly, Congressman Osborne, underage drinking levels, particularly in a targeted segment, remains unacceptably high.

Research conducted by Teenage Research Unlimited and Wirthlin Worldwide for the Century Council revealed additional alarming facts about underage drinking and I think several of you mentioned it in your opening statements today. Sixty-five percent of youth who drink reported obtaining alcohol from family and friends. A separate survey conducted by Wirthlin revealed that a majority of parents believe family and friends are also the leading source of alcohol for today's youth.

Although this number is still unacceptable, it is important to note that this research indicates only 7 percent of youth who drink report obtaining alcohol from a store, bar or club that does not check ID. Other sources include fake IDs and asking strangers outside the store to help them obtain alcohol.

Now encouragingly but indicates that we have a long way to go, research also shows that parents are the most influential factor in a child's decision not to drink. According to recent data such as the 2002 Roper Youth Report, 71 percent of youth identify their parents with having the most influence on their decisions as to whether to drink alcohol or not. Friends and peers are a distant second.

Now these reports confirm the council's longstanding belief that parents are keys to keeping alcohol out of the hands of kids, which is why so many of our programs are directed toward the parents of young people.

Working together, the council believes underage drinking programs should be data-driven, developed by professionals in the field, and why we distribute it to parents, educators and youths.

We are therefore constantly conducting research and evaluation to develop our programs and determine its effectiveness.

Our education efforts are developed by recognized professionals in the education field, reviewed by practitioners and an evaluation is currently built into every program that we implement.

For instance, our Cops and Shops program, implemented in 42 states around the nation, was identified by the Department of Justice publication as a promising practice for reducing attempts for purchase of underage youth. The evaluation found that following the program launch students were more inclined to believe that someone under 21 would be caught and arrested for illegally purchasing beverage alcohol.

Now based on findings, Congressman Osborne that you referred to, which breaks all of our hearts, education now needs to begin as early as 10-years-old. Our newest education program that will be released later this year focuses on middle school students, their parents and educators. Let me assure you that in going to middle schools and developing his agenda, we are working with various government agencies including the United States Department of Education, NIAAA, SAMHSA and the Centers for Disease Control and Prevention.

We are also working with educational groups like the American School Counselors Association, the National Secondary School Principals Association, the National Middle Schools Association, and the National

Latino Children's Institute. We look forward to coming back maybe individually in your office sharing the depth and breadth of these programs with you.

Now as I conclude my remarks, I would like to ask you to watch a very brief PowerPoint presentation we prepared that gives an overview of some of our programs. While they are going on the screen, let me just conclude that we all believe that underage drinking is an issue that requires a sustained response using effective strategies and tactics.

America's leading distillers have from the beginning recognized this fact and have proactively contributed to this activity by contributing to the Century Council through their efforts on the Distilled Spirits Council and their own individual company efforts.

As the Committee attempts to develop strategies to reduce and prevent underage drinking, I thought it important to convey to you what we have done in the past, what we are currently doing and what we will continue to do in the future to ensure that underage drinking is not tolerated.

The Century Council looks forward to working with you, and let me conclude, Chairman, as a member of the Century Council but particularly as a mother of a five and a 7-year old, in these crazy days of much demands on all of your schedule, to all of you who are sitting here today, we are very grateful for your taking a national focus on this problem. Thank you.

[The prepared statement of Ms. Molinari follows:]

Statement of Hon. Susan Molinari, Chairman, the Century Council

Good morning Chairman Castle and other distinguished members of this Committee. My name is Susan Molinari and I am the Chairman of The Century Council.

I am pleased to present testimony to the Committee on this important issue. As a former Member of Congress, it's an honor to be back albeit on the other side of the table.

The Century Council is an independent, national not-for-profit organization dedicated to fighting drunk driving and underage drinking. Headquartered in Washington, D.C., and funded by America's leading distillers, the Council's mission is to promote responsible decision-making regarding drinking, or not drinking, of beverage alcohol and to discourage all forms of irresponsible consumption through education, communications, law enforcement and other programs.

Since 1933, the distilled spirits industry has initiated and supported programs designed to fight alcohol abuse. These programs have spanned throughout the decades.

For example, in the 1960s, the distilled spirits industry funded the development of alcohol education sourcebooks, including Alcohol Education for Classroom and Community for high school and college teachers. Distillers also provided a series of grants to the National Education Association to develop Learning about Alcohol, a popular and widely used text.

In the 1970s, the distillers partnered with the National Football League (NFL) and the Education Commission of the States for several consecutive seasons to co-sponsor national TV and radio messages helping parents educate young people about alcohol. In the 1980s, distillers also partnered with the NFL and the Education Commission of the States to develop Straight Talk about Alcohol, a booklet designed to help parents and teenagers improve their communications on the subject of alcohol. In that decade, distillers also were active sponsors of SADD, Students Against Driving Drunk, and also co-sponsored with DOT the "Friends Don't Let Friends Drive Drunk" campaign.

Formed in 1991, The Council's funding companies (Allied Domecq Spirits & Wine North America, Bacardi USA. Inc., Brown–Forman, DIAGEO, Future Brands LLC, and Pernod Ricard USA) have invested more than $130 million to support the Council's efforts to develop and implement alcohol education and prevention programs.

To date, we have hosted nearly 2,000 events to launch our programs in communities across the nation bringing them to millions of parents, kids, educators, law enforcement officials and traffic safety professionals.

An independent Advisory Board comprised of distinguished leaders in business, government, education, medicine and other relevant disciplines assists the Council in its' development of programs and policies. Additionally, the Council maintains advisory panels in the areas of education and traffic safety that provide related guidance.

The Council's education efforts start in middle school and continue through college. Programs such as Ready or Not, a video-based program utilized in Boys and Girls clubs across the country; Brandon Silveria's, Make the Right Choice, a speaking tour by a young man who was involved in an alcohol-related crash in high school; Parents You're Not Done Yet, a brochure that encourages parents to talk with their kids before they leave for college about the dangers of underage drinking; Cops in Shops a cooperative effort involving local retailers and law enforcement designed to deter minors from attempting to purchase alcohol illegally and adults who purchase alcohol for minors; and Alcohol 101 Plus, an innovative, interactive CD–ROM program aimed at helping students make safe and responsible decisions about alcohol on college campuses are widely used across the country. Other programs such as SPEAK–UP (a joint effort with the National Collegiate Athletic Association), and Promising Practices (a joint effort with George Mason University) and are also in use on our nation's college campuses. In fact, many Members of Congress have participated in and shared these programs with their constituents, such as our Brandon program which is how I was first introduced to The Century Council's good work as a Member of Congress.

Underage drinking is an issue where we must work together. Important progress has been made in reducing underage drinking over the past few decades. The implementation of effective programs has resulted in fewer alcohol-related deaths and injuries among youth but more can be done.

The 2003 Monitoring the Future Study revealed that alcohol consumption was relatively unchanged in 2003, after declining in 2002. Despite the lack of significant decrease in consumption, high school seniors who reported daily drinking in the past month declined 32% proportionally from 70% in 1982 to 48% in 2003. Despite this notable progress, underage drinking levels remain unacceptably high.

Research conducted by Teenage Research Unlimited and Wirthlin Worldwide for The Century Council revealed additional alarming facts about underage drinking in America today: 65 percent of youth who drink report obtaining alcohol from family and friends. A separate survey conducted by Wirthlin revealed a majority of parents believe family and friends are also the leading source of alcohol for today's youth as well.

Although still unacceptable, it is important to note that this research indicates only 7 percent of youth who drink report obtaining alcohol from a store, bar or club that does not check identification. Other sources include fake IDs and asking strangers to buy alcohol.

Research also shows parents are the most influential factor in a child's decision not to drink. According to the last several Roper polls, such as the 2002 Roper Youth Report, 71% of youth identify their parents as having the most influence on their decision whether to drink alcohol or not. Friends and peers are a distant second. These reports confirm The Council's longstanding belief in the important role that parents play in keeping alcohol out of the hands of kids.

The Century Council also believes collective action can have a greater impact than individual efforts. We involve all sectors of the community including beverage alcohol wholesalers and retailers, law enforcement, public officials, educators, insurers, health care professionals and private citizen organizations in the fight against drunk driving and underage drinking.

Working together, the Council also believes underage drinking programs should be data-driven, developed by professionals in the field and widely distributed to parents, educators, and youth. We therefore, constantly conduct research to assist us in developing new programs and to gauge the effectiveness of our efforts.

While many organizations simply identify the problem, identifying the problem is not enough. The Council's education efforts are developed by recognized professionals in the field, reviewed by practitioners, and evaluation is currently built into every program. For instance, our Cops in Shops program, implemented in 42 states around nation, was identified in a Department of Justice publication as a promising practice for reducing attempts to purchase by an underage youth. The evaluation found that following the program launch, students were more inclined to believe that someone under 21 would be caught and arrested for illegally purchasing beverage alcohol.

Alcohol 101 is another example. Requested by more than 1500 college campuses throughout the nation and winner in two categories of the prestigious FREDDIE Awards, Alcohol 101 was recently highlighted in the National Academy of Sciences report as being "independently evaluated with purposeful sampling." The independent evaluation found that the Alcohol 101 CD generates a significant increase in individuals' intent to better regulate their future behavior.

The Council updated and released the successful Alcohol 101 last year in the form of Alcohol 101 Plus an innovative, interactive CD–ROM program aimed at helping students make safe and responsible decisions about alcohol on college campuses. Set on a "virtual campus," Alcohol 101 Plus combines the core elements of the Alcohol 101 program, with new content targeted to at-risk populations—first year students, Greeks, student-athletes, and judicial policy offenders.

The program's realistic scenarios highlight the specific issues, challenges, and decisions these groups face when it comes to alcohol in a college setting and provides students and educators with the opportunity for reflection and discussion. A special edition for high school students is also available to educators nationwide.

All of the Council's programs highlight the need for parents to be involved in the education of today's youth. The Council routinely commissions related research, highlighting issues such as how underage youth access alcohol and when and where alcohol education should be conducted. It is also important to note that many of the Council's programs are available in Spanish and our *Ready or Not* program has a Native American version.

One of the Council's strengths is building effective coalitions for change. Our educational programs have been developed and distributed in cooperation with organizations such as the National Institute on Alcohol Abuse and Alcoholism (NIAAA), the U.S. Department of Education and the National Collegiate Athletic Association (NCAA).

Based on research that says that alcohol education should begin as early as the age of 10, our newest educational program will be released later this year and focuses on middle school students, their parents and educators. In developing this effort, we are working with various government agencies including the U.S. Department of Education, NIAAA, the Substance Abuse and Mental Health Services Administration, and the Centers for Disease Control and Prevention.

We are also working with educational groups such as the American School Counselor Association, the National Secondary School Principals Association, the National Middle School Association, and the National Latino Children's Institute. We look forward to sharing these program materials with you later this year.

Underage drinking is an issue that requires a sustained response using effective strategies and tactics. America's leading distillers have, from the beginning, recognized this fact and have proactively contributed to reducing this activity through The Century Council, The Distilled Spirits Council and their own individual company efforts. As the Committee attempts to develop strategies to reduce and prevent underage drinking, I thought it important to convey to you what we have done in the past, are currently doing and will continue to do in the future to ensure that underage drinking is not tolerated.

I have also enclosed an overview of the Council that provides some background information. The Century Council looks forward to working with you to reduce underage drinking. Once again, thank you for your good work and for the opportunity to testify today.

[Attachments to Ms. Molinari's statement follow:]

Ready or Not: Talking with Kids About Alcohol

- Helps parents and caregivers of middle school aged kids talk about the dangers of underage drinking
- Developed in partnership with the Boys and Girls Clubs of America
- Distributed through over 2000 Boys and Girls Clubs nationwide

THE CENTURY COUNCIL
Funded by America's leading distillers

Brandon Tells His Story

- Talks to high school students about dangers of underage drinking and making good decisions relating to alcohol
- In over 8 years, Brandon's message has reached millions of students across the nation

THE CENTURY COUNCIL
Funded by America's leading distillers

Parents You're Not Done Yet

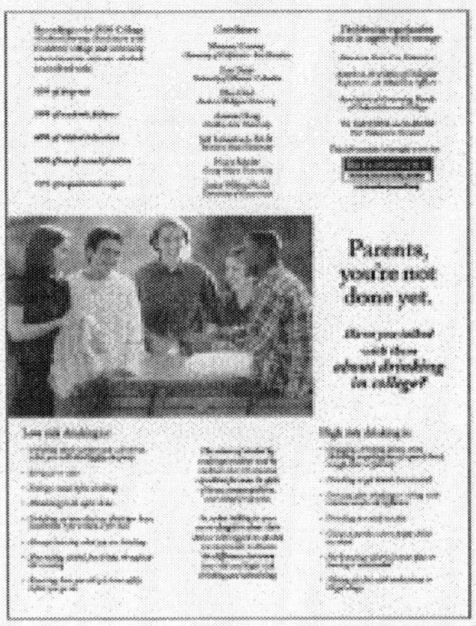

- Designed to encourage parents of college freshman to discuss college drinking before they hit college campuses
- Over 4 million distributed to over 1300 college campuses nationwide

THE CENTURY COUNCIL

Funded by America's leading distillers

Cops in Shops

- Designed to deter minors and adults attempting to purchase for minors using undercover officers posing as clerks
- Implemented in 42 States
- Involves local retailers, law enforcement, educators and media

THE CENTURY COUNCIL

Funded by America's leading distillers

Alcohol 101 Plus

- Designed to encourage college students to make responsible decisions about alcohol
- Over 4000 requests received to date from over 2000 college campuses
- Winner of prestigious Freddie Award
- Alcohol 101 High School version available to educators nationwide

THE CENTURY COUNCIL
Funded by America's leading distillers

Speak Up

- Developed in partnership with NCAA to address alcohol misuse among college athletes
- Utilized by NCAA Champs Life-Skills Coordinators

THE CENTURY COUNCIL
Funded by America's leading distillers

Promising Practices

- First-ever national compilation of effective alcohol education programs and activities on America's college campuses
- Comprehensive program including campus and Task Force planners
- Reviewed and compiled by independent panel of experts led by George Mason University

THE CENTURY COUNCIL
Funded by America's leading distillers

Public Awareness Campaign

- Designed to educate parents about the important role they play in keeping alcohol out of the hands of kids
- Distributing "Tip cards" through alcohol beverage retailers nationwide
- Since August 2003, over 1 million tip cards shared with parents nationwide

THE CENTURY COUNCIL
Funded by America's leading distillers

CENTURY COUNCIL: OVERVIEW AND FACT SHEET

The Century Council, launched in May 1991 and funded by America's leading distillers, is a national, independent not-for-profit organization dedicated to fighting drunk driving and underage drinking and to promoting responsible decision-making regarding beverage alcohol. Since 1991, The Council's funding companies have invested more than $130 million in programs that fight against the misuse of their products.

The Century Council is headquartered in Washington, DC and is chaired by the Honorable Susan Molinari. An independent Advisory Board comprised of distinguished leaders in business, government, education, medicine and other relevant disciplines assist The Council in development of programs and policies.

The Century Council, operating on the philosophy that collective action can have a greater impact than individual efforts, involves all sectors of the community including beverage alcohol wholesalers and retailers, law enforcement, public officials, educators, insurers, health care professionals and private citizen organizations in the fight against drunk driving and underage drinking. For more information, visit www.centurvcouncil.org.

Management

- The Honorable Susan Molinari, Chairman
- Ralph S. Blackman, President and CEO
- William P. Georges, Senior Vice President for Programs

- Maria Harris Tildon, Senior Vice President for External Affairs
- Gordon Anderson, Vice President for Finance

Board Member Companies

- Allied Domecq Spirits & Wine North America
- Bacardi U.S.A., Inc.
- Brown-Forman
- DIAGEO
- Future Brands LLC
- Pernod Ricard USA

Advisory Board

- General Alfred M. Gray, former Commandant, U.S. Marine Corps (Retired)
- Patrick B. Harr, MD, former Chairman of the Board of Directors, American Academy of Family
- Physicians
- The Honorable David C. Miller, Jr., former U.S. Ambassador to Tanzania and Zimbabwe
- Mr. James "Dyke" Nally, President, National Alcohol Beverage Control Association (NABCA)
- George A. Strait, former ABC Medical Correspondent
- S. Frederick Starr, Ph.D. (Fred), Former President of the Aspen Institute and Oberlin College
- The Honorable Ruth Levine Sussman, Justice of the Supreme Court, New York
- The Honorable Togo D. West, Jr., former Secretary of the Army
- Colonel Lonnie J. Westphal, Chief (Ret.) Colorado State Patrol, Former Vice President of IACP

1310 G Street, NW, Suite 600 ■ Washington D.C. 20005
■ Tel 202 637-0077 ■ Facsimile 202 637-0079 www.centurycouncil.org

CORE PROGRAMS

The Council concentrates its efforts in the following areas:

- educating middle school through college students, their parents, teachers, and adult caregivers about the importance of making responsible decisions regarding beverage alcohol;
- informing the public about state laws for blood alcohol concentration (BAC) and how gender, weight, number and type of drink affect an individual's BAC;
- deterring minors from buying beverage alcohol through joint programs with law enforcement and retailers using point of sale materials and public awareness campaigns; and
- reducing drunk driving through research and promising strategies, promoting tougher state and federal legislation, treatment and education.

Education

Ready or Not®: Talking With Kids About Alcohol is a community program created in partnership with Boys & Girls Clubs of America, Ready or Not® helps parents and other adults prevent underage drinking problems among middle-school age children (ages 10 to 14). The program includes a 30-minute video illustrating five concrete steps adults can take to prevent illegal underage drinking and a facilitator kit for use in workshops or at home. Spanish-language *Sin Rodeos®: Hablando con los niños sobre el alcohol* and Native American adaptations are also available free-of-charge.

Brandon Tells His Story is a high school program that features Brandon Silveria, a permanently disabled young man who crashed his car after having a few drinks at age 17. Brandon and his father, Tony, tour America's high schools to educate students — over one million to date — about the dangers and consequences of underage drinking. In addition to the lecture program. The Century Council reaches thousands more students with a half-hour video and accompanying classroom activity guide that brings Brandon's story to high schools across the country. Three video messages focusing on back-to-school, spring break, and prom/graduation are available to keep Brandon's story alive throughout the school year. The video has won the education field's prestigious Chris award and a FREDDIE first-place in the American Medical Association's International Health & Medical Film Competition.

"Parents, You're Not Done Yet" is a brochure designed to encourage parents of incoming college freshmen to discuss college drinking with their kids before they leave home and during the first weeks of the school year. With input from educators, alcohol policy administrators and other higher education professionals, The Council created and has distributed more than 4 million free brochures to over 1,300 colleges. A downloadable version of the brochure, in both English and Spanish, is available online at www.centurycouncil.org.

Alcohol 101 Plus™ is an innovative, interactive CD-ROM program aimed at helping students make safe and responsible decisions about alcohol on college campuses. Set on a "virtual campus," Alcohol 101 Plus combines the core elements of the award-winning Alcohol 101 program, including the "Virtual Bar," with content targeted to at-risk populations — first year students, Greeks, student-athletes, and judicial policy offenders. The realistic scenarios highlight the specific issues, challenges, and decisions these groups face when it comes to alcohol in a college setting and provides students and educators with the opportunity for reflection and discussion. The program includes an interactive alcohol education game developed in partnership with SONY, which teaches the user about how alcohol affects an individual's health, performance, and decision-making. A website, www.alcoholl01plus.org. complements the Alcohol 101 Plus CD by providing a wealth of additional information for students, facilitators, and the media. Alcohol 101 Plus™ received a FREDDIE first-place in the International Health and Medical Awards competition in the category of Health and Wellness, and the program was a finalist in the categories of Community Health and Behavioral Diseases.

Alcohol 101 for High School Seniors is an interactive CD-ROM program with a companion Educator's Guide designed to aid educators in preparing students to make informed choices about alcohol. By demonstrating the negative outcomes of bad decisions and providing safe and healthy alternatives, Alcohol 101 for High School Seniors encourages students to maintain safety and control in situations involving alcohol. Alcohol 101 for High School Seniors was developed through a partnership between the American School Counselor Association (ASCA). Additional information can be found at www.Alcl01forHSseniors.org.

The Blood Alcohol Educator CD-ROM is an interactive CD-ROM for adults that provides the blood alcohol concentration (BAC) limit for driving in a user's particular state and educates the user on how their personal BAC level changes based on their gender, weight and number and type of drink. Once in the program's "Virtual Bar," the user can select from a variety of drinks to determine their BAC level and a clock calculates how long it will take for the user's BAC level to return to zero. The BAE CD-ROM is the centerpiece of a national campaign that includes a BAE Van tour that has distributed over 100,000 BAE CD-ROMs to the public free-of-charge. The BAE Van is outfitted with the colorful BAE logo and builds out into a cyber-cafe with three computer terminals to allow visitors to use the program. The BAE CD-ROM is available in both English and Spanish and, in addition to the CD-ROM and Van tour, can be used on the web at www.b4udrink.org.

Drunk Driving/Traffic Safety

The Century Council believes that only a comprehensive approach to fighting drunk driving, including a blood alcohol concentration of ,08, when accompanied by meaningful BAC education will be effective in reducing alcohol related traffic fatalities.

- *Administrative License Revocation (ALR) laws* — shown to be one of the most effective actions that can be taken to get drunk drivers off the highways. ALR laws require the automatic suspension of the license of a suspected drunk driver who fails or refuses to take a blood alcohol test. The Council has played an important role in passing ALR legislation in Nebraska, New Hampshire, Ohio, Texas, Georgia, Massachusetts and Arkansas.
- *Zero tolerance laws for underage drivers* — set the blood alcohol concentration (BAC) at .02 or less, an amount that prohibits drinking any alcohol at all and driving by a person under 21. Zero tolerance is especially effective when tied to the automatic suspension and loss of license after conviction in court. The Council has helped pass zero tolerance laws in Massachusetts, Georgia, Kentucky, Kansas, Florida, New York, Pennsylvania, Texas and Washington.
- *Hardcore drunk drivers* - these "road predators" represent a small percentage of drivers but are responsible for a disproportionate number of the alcohol-related traffic injuries and fatalities on our nation's highways. These are individuals who drive with a high blood alcohol concentration (BAC) of .15 or above, do so repeatedly as demonstrated by more than one drunk driving arrest, and are highly resistant to changing their behavior. Studies indicated that on any weekend night these recidivist drunk drivers represent less than one percent of the drivers on the road but over 50% of the alcohol-related traffic fatalities at that time.

The Century Council has played a leadership role in the identification of the hardcore drunk driver problem and has developed effective means to combat it. In 1997, The Council launched The National Hardcore Drunk Driving Project, a single, comprehensive resource to assist legislators, highway safety officials, law enforcement officers, judges, prosecutors, community activists and treatment professionals to develop programs that advocate swift identification, certain punishment and effective treatment to reduce hardcore drunk driving. In 2000, The Hardcore Coalition to Fight Drunk Driving was formed as an effort to combine the resources of each organization's similar programs creating synergy in the fight against the hardcore drunk driver. The Coalition includes The Century Council, Mothers Against Drunk Driving (MADD) and the National Transportation Safety Board (NTSB). To download the sourcebook or find more information about our national project, or current legislation, log onto www.dwidata.org.

The Council also has produced a documentary titled "Road Predators" to raise public awareness about hardcore drunk drivers. "Road Predators" aired nationwide on over 120 PBS stations during the months of November and December 1999.

Retailer Programs

- *Point of Sale Materials* - more than ten million posters, decals, buttons and employee information brochures have been distributed free of charge to over 100,000 retailers in all 50 states. Based on recent survey data stating that 65% of youth who drink obtain alcohol from their family and friends, The Century Council, working with the American
- *Beverage Licensees (ABL)*, created a new campaign that highlights the point of access to alcohol by underage youth and encourages parents to play a more active role in keeping alcohol out of the hands of our nation's youth. The key component to the campaign is a 30 second Public Service Announcement, buttons and informational cards, distributed at the point of purchase, that provide tips for parents on how to talk with their kids about alcohol. To raise awareness of the industry's efforts, The Council continues to host local events bringing together retailers, wholesalers, and community leaders to deter underage purchasing.

- *Cops in Shops*®- a cooperative effort, involving local retailers and law enforcement, designed to deter minors from attempting to illegally purchase alcohol and adults who purchase alcohol for minors. Undercover officers are assigned to participating retail locations; often one works inside the store while a second is positioned outside to apprehend adults who procure alcohol for youth. The program is currently being used or has been used in 42 states nationwide.

Hispanic Programs

The Century Council's award-winning Hispanic program –"Si Toma, No Maneje" was the first comprehensive program in the nation to provide the large, growing Hispanic population with Spanish-language anti-alcohol-abuse information. The Century Council's commitment is to provide the Hispanic community with culturally sensitive messages about the dangers of drunk driving and underage drinking. As a result of this approach, The Council has designed a complete array of educational programs that are easy to use and adaptable to the individual needs of the community.

- *¡Hice La Promesa! (I Made the Promise)* - This program, a pledge to not drive drunk, to serve as designated drivers and to encourage families and friends to do the same, was created in partnership with the Catholic Archdiocese of Los Angeles. Over 2,000 parishes have conducted ¡Hice La Promesa! events reaching more than 1 million Catholics.
- *Sin Rodeos: hablando con los ninos sobre el alcohol* — A Spanish language version of The Council's Ready or Not: Talking With Kids About Alcohol program was produced in partnership with the Los Angeles Unified School District (LAUSD). *Sin Rodeos* presents the key messages of *Ready or Not* through culturally

sensitive situations. The program is also supported by the ASPIRA Association, the Cuban American National Council, League of United Latin American Citizens (LULAC), National Association of Latino Elected and Appointed Officials Education Fund (NALEO), National Council of La Raza (NCLR), and the National Puerto Rican Coalition.

- *Public Service Announcements (PSA's)* - In 1994, The Century Council's public service announcement "El Nino" received an award from Hispanic Business Magazine as Best Public Service Announcement.
- *¡Vive, por nuestro futuro! ¡Si tomas, no manejes!* is the title of our most recent campaign developed in partnership with Recording Artists, Actors and Athletes Against Drunk Driving (RADD) and the National Association of Broadcasters (NAB). More than a dozen radio and television PSA's were produced featuring Hispanic celebrities such as: Edward James Olmos, Chayanne, India, Shakira and Tito Puente. The NAB distributed the TV and radio PSAs nationwide in mid-September 2000, in conjunction with Hispanic Heritage Month.
- *Other Programs Available in Spanish* - The Century Council also offers the *Blood Alcohol Educator (BAE) program*, the *"Parents, You're Not Done Yet"* brochure and some *Point of Sale* materials in Spanish.

Public Service Announcements (PSAs)

The Century Council has an ongoing PSA program featuring well-known public figures and celebrities discussing the dangers of drunk driving and the need for alcohol education; many are produced in both English and Spanish.

February 2004

Brandon Quotes

"Brandon and his father's messages were very well received by all the (at-risk) students. It was an especially important message for them to experience firsthand."

Michele M. Ridge
First Lady, Commonwealth of Pennsylvania - Harrisburg, PA

"We can safely say that many young people are alive today because of (Brandon's) good work."

John J. Ring, MD
Past President, American Medical Association

"Life is not a dress rehearsal . . . thanks for bringing that to light for me."

Joel McCarty
Staff Writer, Laurel Leader-Call - Laurel, MS

"Brandon and Tony Silveria are masterful ... their mission in life to assist and educate others is so well done (and) the sincerity of their words are profound and moving. The gift they give so unselfishly is remarkable."

Debbie Derwart
President, Howard Co. MADD - Ellicott City, MD

"One day, when you get to heaven . . . angels will be able to tell you that (because of your story) you saved their life."

Santanna Agee
Student, Mize HS - Mize, MS

"I would recommend the presentation to any organization with members who are old enough to drive. If you get the opportunity ... don't pass it up!

Julia Nichols
Asst. Principal, Bloomington HS - Bloomington, CA

"Thank you for blessing us with your wisdom and openness (in sharing) your story."

Erin Young

Substance Abuse Prevention Specialist, Loudon County Public Schools - Leesburg, VA

"Your story really taught me a lot (and) inspired me not to drink and to avoid peer pressure."

Ryan Heinig

Student, Jenkintown HS - Jenkintown, PA

"Brandon opened the eyes of not only the student body, but also the adult sector in the community. The impact will forever last in (their) minds."

Mark Herrera

Sergeant, Hobbs Police Department - Hobbs, NM

"I've seen lots of videos, had lots of talks, and heard lots of speeches…your story hit me the most!"

Lisa Melchiorre

Student, Davidsen Middle School - Tampa, FL

"I think the realities of (Brandon's) life, shown in such stark detail, will hit home with more impact on the youth who watch this video than any "just say no" type of message ever could."

Carolyn Johnson

Training & Development, Univ. of New Mexico School of Law - Albuquerque, NM

"The core message ... is an inspiration. (Tony and Brandon) received an A+ in my book."

Jack Church

Parent - West, TX

"(Brandon's) honest presentation and genuine concern for others made an impact on our students and staff. Your speech ... inspired and challenged our students and leaders to make the right choices."

Kay Smith
Creekview HS PTSA - Carrolton, TX

"Thank you for sharing your inspirational story with our school. Your elaborate description of your experiences moved us all ... (causing) many people to reconsider how they want to live their lives."

Katherine Aldag
SADD representative, West HS - Madison, WI

"It was clear the students were spellbound . . . you could hear a pin drop. (Brandon's) presentation radiates compassion, a deep commitment to today's youth, and a conviction that they have the power to create their lives through the decisions they make."

Matthew Sinisi
Principal, Memorial HS - West New York, NJ

"One out of a million may not seem like a lot, if you're counting pennies. But by saving one person, you save hundreds of others from grief and suffering. I am inspired."

Stephen McGowan
Student, Fordham Preparatory School - Bronx, NY

"In our society today, in the movies and the musicians around us, show us that drinking is the cool thing to do. They never showed us how hideous the outcomes can be. A hero recovers from mistakes and helps guide others in the right direction. (Brandon) is a hero."

Richelle Brooks
Student, Dansville Central HS - Dansville, NY

"Thank you for making me realize that drinking does have its consequences, and it could ruin everything."

Mia Dinnan
Student, Lapeer West HS - Lapeer, MI

"Though I don't drink now, I am sure (Brandon's) message will stay with me when the pressure is more severe and the opportunity more common."

Elizabeth Birkenmeier

Student, Mary Institute & Saint Louis Country Day School - St. Louis, MO

"Your presentation was very moving and very important. I have talked to many of the kids since the assembly and they all agree that it gave them a lot to think about. You WILL make a difference ... and probably already have!"

Karla Taylor

Principal, Sonora HS - La Habra, CA

"It's bad that people don't listen about the consequences. But when you spoke, everyone listened and realized ... it opened a lot of eyes."

Deirdre Sharpe

Student, Emerson HS - Union City, NJ

"Unlike other lectures, meeting a victim such as (Brandon), and using real images, really stamped any thoughts I had about drinking right out of my mind. It's hard to believe what just two little drinks can do to your life."

Arthur Kim

Student, Issaquah Middle School - Issaquah, WA

"I was crying throughout the assembly. You have inspired me to live life to its fullest."

Kristy Jones

Student, Walton HS - Marietta, GA

"(Our) students witnessed on of the most compelling assembly presentations ever experienced . . . (it) moved students and staff to tears. I have never seen such a tribute in my thirty years of education. I highly recommend (Brandon's) program."

Salvatore Randazzo

Principal, Cheshire HS - Cheshire, CT

"You can be assured that (Brandon) made a difference in the lives of young people that will ripple on for years to come."

Kathy Ward

Coordinator, Youth to Eliminate Loss of Life - Wilmington, DE

"This video will impact numerous young people and save many lives."

Laurie Bello

Detective, Forest Park Police Department - Forest Park, OH

"Please take the time to review ("Brandon Tells His Story") and consider the feasibility of use within your school."

Arlene Cundiff

Safe & Drug-Free Schools Coordinators, Department of Education - Richmond, VA

THE CENTURY COUNCIL

Funded by America's leading distillers

COPS IN SHOPS

Program Information

Cops in Shops®, a cooperative effort involving local retailers and law enforcement, is designed to deter minors from attempting to purchase alcohol illegally and adults who purchase alcohol for minors. Undercover officers are assigned to participating retail locations; one officer works inside the store while a second is positioned outside to apprehend adults who procure alcohol for youth. *Cops in Shops* ® places the focus on the perpetrators — minors who try to purchase alcohol illegally.

Originally tested in four community coalition cities, the program is a primary example of The Century Council's philosophy of developing, testing and then sharing innovative approaches to the problems of drunk driving and illegal underage drinking. The Council makes Cops in Shops ® available to interested communities by providing a "How-To" manual, organizational assistance and point-of-sale and advertising materials.

Cops in Shops® has been implemented in 42 states to date. Here are a few examples of successful programs:

Pennsylvania - Statewide

The Century Council partnered with the Pennsylvania Liquor Control Board and the Pennsylvania Department of Transportation to launch a statewide *Cops in Shops®* program in 1997. The program was supported by a $400,000 grant awarded by the Pennsylvania Department of Transportation. During 1998, program growth into communities statewide made it the largest comprehensive program in the country.

Massachusetts - Statewide

As a result of Massachusetts' 11 successful pilot *Cops in Shops®* programs beginning in 1995, the Massachusetts Governors Highway Safety Bureau allotted over $25,000 in state funds in 1998 to support the expansion of the program. During 1998, *Cops in Shops®* was launched in six new regions involving over 40 communities and the original 11 pilot programs were renewed and expanded. The Massachusetts State Police also received a grant from the U.S. Department of Justice to support *Cops in Shops®* programs in more rural sections of the state beginning in April 1999. To date, The Century Council has partnered with Massachusetts' Alcohol Beverage Commission, Governor's Highway Safety Office and many individual law enforcement agencies to launch and revitalize *Cops in Shops®*.

Atlanta, Georgia

The Georgia Sheriffs Association, along with 13 sheriff departments in the Atlanta area and The Century Council, introduced *Cops in Shops®* to the Metro- Atlanta area in 1997. Due to the positive impact of *Cops in Shops®* in the 13 counties, several Georgia sheriff and police departments have contacted the Council seeking assistance in launching their *Cops in Shops®* programs. Throughout 1998 the program expanded and today, Georgians can find Cops in Shops m in a majority of the state's counties.

Virginia

After a very successful *Cops in Shops®* program in parts of Virginia during 1997, program partners focused on creating a statewide campaign. In mid- 1998, the Virginia Attorney General's Office, Virginia Governor's Office, Virginia Department of Alcoholic Beverage Control and several other Virginia organizations joined The Century Council to launch the third phase of Cops in Shops ® in central Virginia.

Tampa/St. Petersburg, Florida

Cops in Shops® was originally launched in February 1996, through a cooperative effort between the Tampa Police Department, St. Petersburg Police Department, Pinellas County Sheriff's Department, Hillsborough County Sheriff's Department and nearly 4,000 alcohol retailers.

The program is currently maintained and operated by the Hillsborough and Pinellas county sheriff's departments. *Cops in Shops®* materials were redistributed in December 1996, to re-energize program partners and raise community awareness.

Dallas, Texas

The Century Council launched the *Cops in Shops®* program in partnership with the Dallas Police Department, Texas Alcoholic Beverage Commission and Texas Department of Transportation in June 1995. An estimated 600 retailers participate in the ongoing program.

In February 1996, the Council launched the *Cops in Shops®* program in Plano, a suburb of Dallas.

The program is a cooperative effort of the Plano Police Department, Texas Alcoholic Beverage Commission and more than 100 retailers.

Houston, Texas

Following the successful launch of the Dallas *Cops in Shops*® program, The Century Council, in partnership with the Houston Police Department, Harris County Sheriff's Department, Texas Alcoholic Beverage Commission and Texas Department of Transportation launched the program in 1996. More than 3,500 retailers participated in the ongoing program.

THE CENTURY COUNCIL

Funded by America's leading distillers

BRANDON SILVERIA EDUCATIONAL PROGRAM

Facts-at-a-Glance

Description

Brandon Silveria is a young man, who at age 17, was involved in a near fatal crash after drinking at a high school party. After enduring a coma for nearly three months and another three years of painful rehabilitation, Brandon and his father Tony tour America's high schools full-time on behalf of The Century Council. Despite his permanent and visible speech and walking disabilities, Brandon delivers a compelling message to teens about the dangers of drinking and driving. To date, Brandon's life-saving message has reached over one million students.

Media

In addition to local media coverage in every city Brandon visits, his story has been featured on nationally syndicated "*Rescue 911*" and "*Leeza.*" NBC's "*Today Show*" developed a special segment on the Silverias which was aired to coincide with prom and graduation season.

Program Areas

Supporting Educational Materials

To reach the greatest number of students with the Silverias' message, a compelling 30-minute video, called "Brandon's Story," and supporting curriculum materials are available free of charge in areas where the Silverias are not able to appear in person. Honored with the American Medical Association's prestigious 11 FREDDIE 'Award, the video can also be used to precede or follow a Silveria visit. Taped audio and video "reminders" are available to schools for use on the public address or closed circuit television systems to prompt students to remember Brandon's message and Make the Right Choice at critical periods such as prom time and spring break.

The Century Council

The Century Council is a national not-for-profit organization dedicated to fighting alcohol abuse, concentrating on drunk driving and underage drinking. The Council was founded in 1991 and is funded by America's leading distillers.

Contact Information

The Century Council
1310 G Street, NW, Suite 600
Washington, DC 20005
202-637-0077
www.centurycouncil.org

To email Brandon Silveria, please visit www.centurycouncil.org/brandon.

THE CENTURY COUNCIL

Funded by America's leading distillers

The Century Council believes that collective action brings about lasting change.

Operating under this philosophy, the Council promotes action through strategic partnerships with various public and private groups and organizations including;

- National Middle School Association
- National School Boards Association
- National Congress of American Indians
- American School Counselor Association
- National Association of Secondary School Principals
- National Collegiate Athletic Association
- National Interfraternity Council
- National Panhellenic Conference
- Bacchus & Gamma Peer Education Network
- American Council on Education
- Hispanic Association of Colleges and Universities
- American Association of Collegiate Registrars and Admissions Officers
- Centers for Disease Control and Prevention
- United States Department of Education
- National Institute on Alcohol Abuse and Alcoholism
- American Academy of Family Physicians

- National Latino Children's Institute
- Substance Abuse and Mental Health Services Administration
- George Mason University
- Governors Highway Safety Association
- National Alcohol Beverage Control Association
- International Association of Chiefs of Police
- National Commission Against Drunk Driving
- Mothers Against Drunk Driving
- National Transportation Safety Board
- National Association of State Judicial Educators

THE CENTURY COUNCIL

Funded by America's leading distillers

ALCOHOL 101 PLUS™

Facts-at-a-Glance

The Century Council designed Alcohol 101 Plus, an interactive CD-ROM program, to help prevent the misuse of alcohol on college campuses. Using SONY game technology and set on a "virtual campus," Alcohol 101 Plus specifically targets at-risks populations of the student body: First Year students, Greeks, student-athletes, and judicial policy offenders. Through interactive video scenarios and using 3D animation, users have the opportunity to make "virtual" decisions for "virtual" characters.

Representing an over million dollars investment, the creation of Alcohol 101 Plus brought about a broad alcohol industry-government partnership designed to prevent the misuse of alcohol on college campuses including the U.S. Department of Education; National Institute of Alcohol Abuse and Alcoholism, and U.S. Department of Health and Human Services. Additionally, more than 50 on-campus practitioners, student focus groups, as well as representatives from the National Collegiate Athletic Association (NCAA); and The BACCHUS and GAMMA Peer Education Network participated in the creative and content development of the program.

Alcohol 101 Plus is a primary example of The Century Council's philosophy of developing, testing, and then sharing innovative approaches to the problems of drunk driving and underage drinking, especially on college campuses. The Council makes Alcohol 101 Plus available free-of-charge to interested communities by providing the CD-ROM, a facilitator's guide, and support materials which can be ordered online at www.alcohol 101 plus.org.

The Century Council is a national, not-for-profit organization dedicated to developing educational programs to fight drunk driving and underage drinking. The Council was founded in 1991 and is funded by America's leading distillers.

"Ready or Not®: Talking with Kids About Alcohol"

What It Is

Ready or Not is an innovative and timely video educational program to help parents and adults who work with middle school children (ages 10 to 14) prevent illegal underage drinking. *Ready or Not* is a community program of The Century Council in partnership with Boys & Girls Clubs of America.

In addition to the original English version, *Ready or Not* is available in two culturally sensitive editions - a Spanish language version titled *Sin*

Rodeos®: hablando con los ninos sobre el alcohol and a special American Indian adaptation. Both adaptations were developed with leaders from those communities. There is also a captioned version of the videotape created for the hearing impaired. All versions are offered free of charge.

What It Does

The program helps adults understand the role of alcohol in middle school children's lives; assess their own behavior and attitudes toward alcohol, and how these can affect children; and learn five common-sense strategies to help prevent children from drinking illegally.

How It Works

Ready or Not is centered around a half-hour video that includes real-life interviews with kids talking to adults about alcohol; interviews with child psychologists and alcohol abuse experts; and five realistic prevention scenarios showing adults and children in situations involving alcohol. The video can be viewed in privacy at home or adults can participate in 60- to 90-minute group workshops run by facilitators.

Evaluation Results

In March 1995 the Pacific Institute for Research and Evaluation (PIRE) conducted an independent evaluation of Ready or Not. Focus group and survey results indicated that two-thirds of the parents increased their discussions about alcohol with their children in the four to six weeks following the program. Two-thirds of those parents found the program helpful in deciding what to say. In addition, many reported that the program increased their awareness, not only of the problem of middle-school-age drinking, but of the mixed messages adults who abuse alcohol send to children.

Program Materials

The *Ready or Not* program consists of several elements:

- A 30-minute video
- A participant's brochure that summarizes the program's five key prevention strategies
- A comprehensive Facilitator's Kit for use in group workshops. The kit includes:
  - A facilitator's guide
  - Dilemma cards sketching hypothetical situations in which an adult might be confronted with alcohol-related issues in their child's life
  - Invitation flyers for group workshops
  - Feedback cards for both workshop participants and facilitators

All program materials, including the video, can be reproduced by supporting organizations for repeated use and publicity purposes.

January 2001

* * *

A Word About Cultural Sensitivity

Both the American Indian adaptation and *Sin Rodeos: hablando con los niños sobre el alcohol*, present the key messages of *Ready or Not* in a manner that is both culturally appropriate and relevant. The Council worked very closely with experts and representatives from within the community to ensure the quality and relevance of the program.

The American Indian version features two new video scenarios filmed with Indian actors and dialogue that includes the themes of trust and respect. All materials and packaging incorporate images of Indian children and traditional symbols. For example, the dilemma cards were modified to put the reader into realistic situations as may be found on reservations and in Indian homes. This version was recently endorsed by the National Congress of American Indians through a formal resolution passed at their annual session.

The *Sin Rodeos* video was produced entirely in Spanish using language and situations that are relevant and representative of the diversity within the Hispanic community. All materials and packaging feature Latino images and accurate cultural themes. *Sin Rodeos* has the support of many organizations, including the National Council of La Raza and the National Association of Latino Elected and Appointed Officials.

* * *

Mr. Osborne. [Presiding] Thank you very much.

I would like to remind the witnesses that they have 5 minutes and you have a green light, a yellow light comes on when you have 1 minute left, and the red light is at 5 minutes, so we would appreciate it if you would try to adhere to those timelines. Bob.

STATEMENT OF ROBERT L. NEWTON, DIRECTOR, BUSINESS DEVELOPMENT, BETTY FORD CENTER, RANCHO MIRAGE, CALIFORNIA

Mr. Newton. I guess it's Mr. Vice Chairman and Subcommittee members, good morning. I have a hard time not calling you "Coach," so excuse me. For 36 years I have been calling you that.

I am very appreciative of that.

I am very grateful to be here this morning and on behalf of the Betty Ford Center and the Partnership for Recovery. As Coach Osborne was sharing some of my background, I did play in the NFL for 11 years for the Bears and the Seahawks, and after a distinguished college career at the University of Nebraska. I was released from the Seahawks in September, 1982, excuse me.

In July 1983 I was admitted to an alcoholism/drug treatment center in Monroe, Washington, diagnosed as a late stage alcoholic/drug addict. That first week I was in that treatment center at age 33, I was extremely in shock. One of the aspects that I learned in that treatment center is at age 13 is when I had my first beer. It was a Saturday afternoon, and my best friend offered it to me that he had stolen from his parents. I didn't know how to get out of that situation, and that was the first instance that I felt peer pressure.

I had a few more beers that day, and I ended up getting very sick and it was a very toxic chemical to my body, but I failed to heed that warning. I went into high school and I continued to drink heavily with my friends, and I was raised with a lot of mixed messages.

My father had a severe problem with alcohol, as did most of my uncles on my mother's and father's side. Alcoholism was very prevalent in my family. All the men drink. It was a mixed message to me. I thought drinking alcohol, especially beer, had something to do with being a man and being mature.

I continued this behavior and got my first DUI at age 17. I ended up getting more, several DUIs. I am very grateful today that I didn't kill somebody under the influence of alcohol.

Also when I was in that treatment center, I became aware of how ignorant our society is about alcohol problems and alcoholism. I kind of made a commitment that one of these days—I was in treatment—that I was going to try to help educate people about alcohol problems and alcoholism and drug addiction.

I became a certified counselor in 1988 and I started working in schools. I went to many schools and gave many presentations and seminars, trying to build awareness about alcohol and other drugs.

I heard a lot of statistics this morning and they were very, very well presented. But one of the ones I came across, preparing for this, is that 38 percent of eighth grade female girls who attempted suicide were heavy drinkers of alcohol, versus 11 percent of eighth grade girls who did not drink alcohol. I think it is very obvious young people do not understand that alcohol is a very powerful depressant on the nervous system and a very powerful drug.

A lot of times I hear that parents are responsible. We've got 6 million kids living with an impaired parent that has a problem with alcohol or drug addiction. There's no way they are going to get an understanding, a clear message that is going to prevent them from using.

One of the reasons that I used alcohol is to help me with the emotional turmoil I was having with my father because of his drinking.

A lot of you said, well, Bob, did alcohol hurt you? I mean, you went on and played for Nebraska, and you played in the NFL. I never reached my potential as a football player. Alcohol caused major negative legal consequences in my life, with DUIs. It was a major contributor to a divorce, and financial ruin. So it did impair my life, even though I played football for a long time.

As a student assistance program counselor for a local high school in Tacoma, Washington, I came—I was able to observe many young kids get help with early intervention and I can't tell you—a lot of these kids were coming from families that had alcohol problems and they had a chance to get counseling and treatment.

A lot of these kids, as Coach Osborne mentioned, were addicted already at 15 or 16 years old, and I have seen kids as young as 12 having a severe problem with addiction with alcohol and other drugs. I just feel our society is continuing to send a mixed message to children, to young people. I don't like that alcohol and sports are interrelated in every sporting event. I think that is the wrong message for young people. I never saw alcohol improve an athlete's career. I did see alcohol ruin many athletes' careers.

To sum up, what would I suggest to Congress, what we can do?

You know, inaction is not working. Not taking action is hurting us.

We need to—I am in full support of the NAS recommendations, especially that we have a Federal strategy for prevention and intervention to help young people and an excise tax to alcohol to help the media campaign to educate our society, especially adults, because as Wendy said, a lot of the alcohol is accessed through parents and adults, and so they need as much education as our adolescents.

I thank you for having me here today. Thank you very much.

[The prepared statement of Mr. Newton follows:]

Statement of Robert L. Newton, Director, Business Development, Betty Ford Center, Rancho Mirage, California

The Betty Ford Center is a non-profit licensed addiction hospital in Rancho Mirage, California. Mrs. Ford opened the facility in October 1982 to help those suffering from alcoholism and other drug addiction and their families. The center has helped over 61,000 people since its opening. Levels of care provided at the Betty Ford center include: inpatient care, residential day treatment, and intensive outpatient services. We have specialty programs including our licensed professional program, family and children's programs.

The Substance Abuse and Mental Health Services Administration (SAMHSA) reports that more than 6 million children live with at least one parent who abuses or is dependent on alcohol or an illicit drug. The Betty Ford Center's Children's Program attempts to help children whose parents have struggled with addiction by providing a program where they can learn problem-solving, coping and self-care strategies.

The Betty Ford Center is a member of the Partnership for Recovery (PFR), a public policy coalition comprised of nine of the nation's leading alcohol and drug addiction treatment providers and the field's trade association, the National Association of Addiction Treatment Providers

(NAATP). Members include: the Betty Ford Center, Bradford Health Systems, Caron Foundation, Cumberland Heights, Father Martin's Ashley, Gateway Rehabilitation Center, Hazelden Foundation, NAATP, Sierra Tucson, and Valley Hope Association. The PFR was formed in 1997 because the Centers share a common philosophy in the treatment and care of individuals and their families suffering from chemical dependency and share a common interest in shaping policy that affects those in or seeking recovery. The treatment providers offer a continuum of care including traditional and intensive outpatient, residential inpatient, day or partial care and sub-acute detoxification. Each PFR facility also utilizes American Society of Addiction Medicine (ASAM) Patient Placement criteria to determine admission, length of stay and discharge for all levels of care.

Background

I have worked in the chemical dependency field since 1986 as a counselor, educator, and administrator. I have been a CADC [certified alcohol drug counselor] since 1988. I currently work at the Betty ford center as a business development associate and counselor. I've also worked in many school systems presenting numerous lectures and seminars regarding prevention and intervention to substance use for students, teachers, administrators and coaches. Some of my work with youth included SAP [Student Assistance Program] counseling for a high school in Tacoma, WA., where I evaluated adolescents for chemical use, provided individual counseling and family education. This work also included training teachers, administrators and coaches about signs and symptoms of chemical use problems in the school. The SAP experience was extremely insightful and a valuable experience. I was able to provide early intervention for numerous young people experiencing alcohol and other drug abuse and/or addiction. This early intervention gave the young person an opportunity to seek counseling and/or treatment. I observed many young people turn their lives around from the SAP process. I have great concern that the Student Assistance Program is diminishing throughout the country because of budget woes. Many young people will suffer from not having an SAP on every high school and middle school campus.

The Seattle Seahawks football team also utilized my services as a consultant regarding their alcohol/drug programs. I provided evaluations, individual counseling and trainings for players and staff and treatment recommendations. My past work also included evaluation specialist and educator for the University of Nebraska athletic department.

Prior to my work in the chemical dependency field I played in the National Football League for eleven years as an offensive lineman with the Chicago Bears [1971–1975] and Seattle Seahawks [1976–1981]. I was a team member on the first national Championship college football team for the University of Nebraska in 1970. I was also honored as a consensus All–American offensive tackle in 1970.

My NFL career ended in 1982 because of my alcoholism and other drug dependencies. I entered alcoholism treatment in July 1983 and I'm very grateful that I have been clean and sober since July 12, 1983. One of the aspects I learned about my alcoholism while I was in treatment is the mixed messages I received as a young teenager about alcohol use. I had my first drink of alcohol [beer] at age 13 as a result of peer pressure from one of my friends. I had a few other beers that afternoon and became very sick. But I did not heed this warning and continued to drink through high school because I felt drinking alcohol had something to do with being mature and being a man. Again, I had received confusing messages about alcohol from my friends and alcohol advertisements and did not have the leadership at home from my family because my dad had a severe problem with alcohol. Although I had a successful college football career and played a long time in the NFL, I never played up to my potential and alcohol use caused me to be cut from the Seahawks.

Alcohol caused major legal problems in my life regarding DUI'S. I had my first DUI at age seventeen. Alcohol was a big factor in my divorce and severely impaired my physical and mental health.

The Scope of the Underage Drinking Problem

Today I feel our young people are still receiving mix messages regarding alcohol.

Underage drinking is a serious widespread problem in America that deserves immediate Congressional action. Approximately 10.7 million underage Americans, 28.8 % of the 12 to 20 age group, reported drinking alcohol in the month prior to being surveyed by the 2002 National Survey on Drug Use and Health and 7.2 million of those teens are classified as binge drinkers.[2] Furthermore, underage drinkers are responsible for almost 20% of all alcohol consumed in the United States, with $22.5 billion spent on alcohol in 1999.[3]

Teens and adults incorrectly view alcohol as less harmful than other drugs and, while many Americans view teen drinking as a right of passage, we cannot ignore the serious long and short-term consequences associated with illegal underage drinking.

Underage Drinking and Illicit Drug Use Are Inextricably Linked to Youth Sexual Assault and Suicide

As I can tell you first hand, underage drinking and alcohol abuse can result in serious negative consequences in the lives of our nation's youth. Early experimentation with alcohol puts teens at a greater risk for developing a problem with alcohol and/or substance abuse. A study released just last month found that the basis for adult substance abuse has been generally established for a person by the time he or she finishes high school.[4] Youth who begin drinking before age 15 are four times likelier to

---

[2] Department of Health and Human Services, Substance Abuse and Mental Health Services Administration. (2003). *2002 National Survey on Drug Use and Health*.

[3] Susan E. Foster, et al, "Alcohol Consumption and Expenditures for Underage Drinking and Adult Excessive Drinking," *Journal of the American Medical Association*. (February 2003): 289:989–995.

[4] Alicia Merline, et al, "Substance Use among Adults 35 Years of Age: Prevalence, Adulthood Predictors, and Impact of Adolescent Substance Use," *American Journal of Public Health*. (January 2004).

develop alcohol dependence than those who begin drinking at age 21.[5] Furthermore, alcohol use strongly associates with illicit drug use and 30.7% of heavy drinkers aged 12 and older concurrently use illicit drugs.[6] Thus, the Partnership for Recovery and the Betty Ford Center applaud the Office of National Drug Control Policy (ONDCP)'s new ad campaign that debuted during the Super Bowl that links youth alcohol consumption with substance abuse. ONDCP reports that this ad ranked as the number one Super Bowl ad among viewers aged 17 and under and we hope that additional ads will be forthcoming.

Underage drinking can damage developing brains and put our children at higher risk for sexual assault and suicide. For example, one study found that 37% of eighth grade females who drank heavily reported attempting suicide, compared with 11% who did not drink. NIAAA reports that "underage alcohol use is more likely to kill young people than all illegal drugs combined[7] and in 2002, 24% of drivers ages15 to 20 years old who were killed in crashes were intoxicated.[8] We need to tackle this problem before it destroys or ends the lives of any more American children.

The Economic Consequences of Underage Drinking

The economic consequences associated with underage drinking are staggering.

The Institute of Medicine and National Research Council (IOM/NRC) report released last September found that underage drinking costs the nation an estimated $53 billion annually in losses stemming from traffic fatalities, violent crime, and other behaviors that threaten the well-being of

[5] National Institute on Alcohol Abuse and Alcoholism, National Institutes of Health. (1998) *NIH News Release.*

[6] Department of Health and Human Services, Substance Abuse and Mental Health Services Administration. (2003). *2002 National Survey on Drug Use and Health.*

[7] National Institute on Alcohol Abuse and Alcoholism. (2003) *Alcohol Alert.*

[8] National Highway Traffic Safety Administration, U. S Department of Transportation. *Traffic Safety Facts 2002: Young Drivers*. (2003)

America's youth.[9] If this cost were shared equally by each congressional district, the amount would approximately total more than $120 million per district.[10]

Recommendations

Congress has the opportunity to help curtail underage drinking—a problem that will not go away on its own. The IOM/NRC report made several recommendations on necessary steps to reduce underage drinking. The Betty Ford Center and the PFR urge Congress to act as swiftly as possible to enact these recommendations.

While I realize that not all of the recommendations are within the purview of this Committee, I believe they deserve Congressional attention.

Reform Advertising

- Alcohol companies, advertising companies, and commercial media should refrain from marketing practices (including product design, advertising, and promotional techniques) that have substantial underage appeal and should take reasonable precautions in the time, place, and manner of placement and promotion to reduce youthful exposure to other alcohol advertising and marketing activity
- The alcohol industry trade associations, as well as individual companies, should strengthen their advertising codes to preclude placement of commercial messages in venues where a significant proportion of the expected audience is underage, to prohibit the use of commercial messages that have substantial underage appeal, and

---

[9] Richard Bonnie, et al. *Reducing Underage Drinking: A Collective Responsibility* (September 2003). National Research Council & Institute of Medicine.

[10] David Levy, et al, (1999) *Costs of Underage Drinking* U.S. Department of Justice.

to establish independent external review boards to investigate complaints and enforce the codes

- Congress should appropriate the necessary funding for the U.S. Department of Health and Human Services to monitor underage exposure to alcohol advertising on a continuing basis and to report periodically to Congress and the public. The report should include information on the underage percentage of the exposed audience and estimated number of underage viewers of print and broadcasting alcohol advertising in national markets and, for television and radio broadcasting, in a selection of large local or regional markets *FUND HHS UNDERAGE DRINKING MEDIA CAMPAIGN*
- The federal government should fund and actively support the development of a national media effort, as a major component of an adult-oriented campaign to reduce underage drinking
- Intensive research and development for a youth-focused national media campaign relating to underage drinking should be initiated. If this work yields promising results, the inclusion of a youth-focused campaign in the strategy should be reconsidered

Develop a Federal Strategy to Prevent Underage Drinking

- A federal interagency coordinating committee on prevention of underage drinking should be established, chaired by the secretary of the U.S. Department of Health and Human Services
- The annual report of the secretary of the U.S. Department of Health and Human Services on underage drinking should include key indicators of underage drinking
- The Monitoring the Future (MTF) Survey and the National Household Survey on Drug Use and Health (NSDUH) should be revised to elicit more precise information on the quantity of alcohol consumed and to ascertain brand preferences of underage drinkers

Raise Alcohol Excise Taxes

- Congress and state legislatures should raise excise taxes to reduce underage consumption and to raise additional revenues for this purpose. Top priority should be given to raising beer taxes, and excise tax rates for all alcoholic beverages should be indexed to the consumer price index so that they keep pace with inflation without the necessity of further legislative action *SUPPORT COMMUNITY MOBILIZATION EFFORTS*
- Community leaders should assess the underage drinking problem in their communities and consider effective approaches—such as community organizing, coalition building, and the strategic use of the mass media—to reduce drinking among underage youth
- Public and private funders should support community mobilization to reduce underage drinking. Federal funding for reducing and preventing underage drinking should be available under a national program dedicated to community-level approaches to reducing underage drinking, similar to the Drug Free Communities Act, which supports communities in addressing substance abuse with targeted, evidence-based prevention strategies

Strengthen Law Enforcement Efforts

- States should strengthen their compliance check programs in retail outlets, using media campaigns and license revocation to increase deterrence
- States and localities should implement enforcement programs to deter adults from purchasing alcohol for minors
- States should facilitate enforcement of zero tolerance laws in order to increase their deterrent effect
- Local police, working with community leaders, should adopt and announce policies for detecting and terminating underage drinking parties I understand that Representatives Frank Wolf (R–VA),

> Lucille Roybal–Allard (D–CA), and Zach Wamp (R–TN) intend to introduce legislation containing a Office of Public Health and Science and U.S. Surgeon General funded media campaign aimed at reducing underage drinking. From my own experience, I know that such a campaign would be invaluable for the millions of American youth who are bombarded with mixed messages about drinking.

On behalf of the Betty Ford Center and the Partnership for Recovery, thank you for the opportunity to testify today on such an important issue affecting America's youth. We look forward continuing to work with Congress to reduce and prevent underage drinking. Thank you.

Mr. Osborne. Thanks, Bob. Ms. Hamilton.

STATEMENT OF WENDY J. HAMILTON, NATIONAL PRESIDENT, MOTHERS AGAINST DRUNK DRIVING

Mrs. HAMILTON. Thank you, Mr. Chairman, Vice Chairman Osborne, and Ranking Member Woolsey for holding this important hearing today. My name is Wendy Hamilton. I am the National President of Mothers Against Drunk Driving. MADD's mission is to stop drunk driving, support the victims of this violent crime, and prevent underage drinking. I am honored to be here testifying on this critical public health issue. Your leadership is going to be very important in identifying systemic changes that will keep our children safe.

This is a historic time. With the recent release of the National Academy of Sciences report, Congress is developing a strategy to prevent underage drinking. The NAS and the nation's top public health researchers examined the problem and my comments today will focus on NAS's science-based solutions to save lives.

Alcohol is the illegal drug of choice for America's youth, with 10.1 million underage drinkers in this nation. Alcohol is a major factor in the three leading causes of death of America's teens. Forty-nine percent of high school seniors reported drinking in the last 30 days, more than those using marijuana or tobacco combined, and for over a decade underage drinking rates have flatlined.

I have submitted for the record a sheet from Monitoring the Future data, which shows that since 1991 this number has not moved.

In over 10 years it has not moved.

Teens have easy access to alcohol. They are saturated with irresponsible alcohol ads. Underage drinking laws are not well-enforced and communities often look the other way. The consequences of underage drinking are staggering. Research demonstrates that the younger children begin to drink alcohol, the more likely they are to become alcohol dependent or drive drunk later in life.

Young drivers constitute 13 percent of the alcohol-involved drivers in fatal crashes and individuals under 21 commit over a third of all rapes, robberies and assaults. Half of this is alcohol-related.

Neuroscience documents that the adolescent brain develops into the early 20's and youth alcohol use stunts physical development and functioning of the brain. In addition to the human toll, the NAS concluded that the $53 billion price tag appears to be an underestimate of the social costs of underage drinking.

In fiscal 2000 the Nation spent approximately $1.8 billion on preventing illicit drug use, but only $71.1 million on underage drinking prevention. A 2001 GAO report confirmed that the government's approach is disjointed and that only 7 percent of total Federal funds available for alcohol and other drug prevention focused on underage drinking.

MADD supports NAS Recommendation 12-1 for a Federal interagency coordinating committee to align Federal efforts to prevent underage drinking, and the Department of Education must be a key player. NAS reports that education-oriented interventions should be implemented within a comprehensive approach, and MADD supports NAS Recommendation 6-1, which encourages the government to develop a national media campaign to reduce underage drinking that targets adults. Most adults including parents underestimate the dangers of underage drinking and even facilitate children's drinking by allowing access to alcohol.

This media campaign is necessary to elevate and frame this important issue. Youth who drink remember 10 percent less of what they have learned than those who don't drink. Higher absenteeism rates and lower GPAs are associated with great alcohol use.

The Safe and Drug Free Schools program is the Federal Government's primary vehicle for reducing drug, alcohol, tobacco use and violence. Currently the state grants program has lower funding levels than 1991. The administration's fiscal year 2005 request contains $441 million for state grants, $28 million less than 2003. The 2005 budget request proposes a $30 million slash in alcohol prevention programming, cutting the only K through 12 money within Safe and Drug Free Schools that targets alcohol prevention.

Making underage drinking prevention programs optional for schools is a major flaw in our system. This Committee has the opportunity to establish stable ongoing funding for prevention programs committed to reducing underage drinking. MADD supports NAS Recommendation 10-2, which urges HHS and DOE to fund only evidence-based education interventions. MADD applauds the rigorous standards required by SAMHSA and the DOE for programs seeking eligibility into the national registry of effective programs. MADD worked very hard to ensure the effectiveness of its elementary school program, Protecting You, Protecting Me, an alcohol use prevention curriculum for Grades 1 through 5, was named a model program by HHS and is on the national registry of effective programs.

Scientific evaluation of PYPM has shown that students receiving the lessons are more knowledgeable of their brains, more media literate, less likely to ride with a driver who has been drinking, and less likely to drink as teens.

Continued growth of this and other proven programs is necessary as we seek to create a culture where underage drinking is not a rite of passage. There has to be a long-term commitment to evaluation to ensure that tax dollars are being spent on programs that work.

School-based programs have only modest results if not coupled with research-based community prevention interventions.

MADD designed Youth in Action as a community initiative where students work on projects proven to reduce underage drinking. These teams work to change the community environment that condones underage drinking, from the store clerk that doesn't check IDs to the adults willing to buy beer for kids.

Young people have to learn about alcohol in the classroom but must also be engaged in community interactions and we urge this Committee to allow community-based programs like Youth in Action to be accepted as model programs.

The alcohol industry has relied on unevaluated, unproven programs to combat underage drinking. NAS reports that it is aware of only one industry-sponsored education program that has been independently evaluated and further research was suggested on that particular program.

It found that the rest of the industry's material had no backing in science.

Underage drinkers consume between $11-22 billion worth of alcohol annually. When else would we trust a manufacturer to convince customers not to buy their products? Yet for underage drinking, many are willing to leave the sole education of our children to the alcohol industry. The alcohol industry has not created programs that stand up to scientific scrutiny.

If we don't put an end to the complacent attitude about underage drinking we continue to put our children in harm's way. Many would like to blame parents for this problem, but they are just a piece of the puzzle.

Kids are growing up where alcohol is easy to get, irresponsible advertising is everywhere, and underage drinking laws are not well enforced. I remember, and I'm sure most of this Committee knows, what it is like to have a child leave on a Friday night and just pray that they get home safely. That's what I did every Friday.

Our nation can no longer pretend that underage drinking is a mere rite of passage and harmless. Our children deserve more, and as a parent and an activist forever changed by the devastation caused by a drunk driver, I urge this Committee to embrace the role that you play in expanding youth and community interventions through the educational system. Thank you.

[The prepared statement of Mrs. Hamilton follows:]

Statement of Wendy J. Hamilton, National President, Mothers against Drunk Driving

Good Morning. My name is Wendy Hamilton and I am the National President of Mothers Against Drunk Driving. MADD's mission is to stop drunk driving, support the victims of this violent crime and prevent underage drinking. I am honored to be here today to testify on the critical public health issue of illegal youth alcohol use.

I would like to take this opportunity to thank Chairman Castle, Vice Chairman Osborne, Ranking Member Woolsey and the entire Subcommittee for holding this hearing today. Your leadership will be so important in identifying systemic changes that will help keep our children safe from harms caused by underage alcohol use.

Despite the fact that alcohol kills six and a half times more youth than all other illicit drugs combined, there has been minimal attention paid to this public health issue. However, it is a historic time in our nation. With the release of the Congressionally mandated National Academy of Sciences/Institute of Medicine (NAS) September 2003 report titled "Reducing Underage Drinking, A Collective Responsibility," Congress has started working toward the development of a comprehensive strategy to prevent underage drinking. The NAS assembled the nation's top public health researchers to examine a problem that has been overlooked for far too long.

Many of my comments today will focus on the NAS recommendations as the report offers proven, science-based solutions that, if implemented, will save young lives.

The public health and safety communities have been pursuing action at the federal level for many years on this issue, but only now has the necessary national dialogue begun. The NAS report provides a groundbreaking opportunity to help put the nation's number one youth drug problem on the national policy agenda and gives our nations' leaders the impetus for concrete action. All of the NAS recommendations should be seriously considered by Congress, the Administration, and state and local leaders. While MADD supports the NAS report in its entirety, my remarks will focus on areas in which this committee can have the greatest impact. I applaud your commitment to shine the national spotlight on this sorely neglected issue.

Overview of the Problem

Without question, alcohol is the most widely used drug among America's youth.

It is illegal for people under the age of 21 to drink alcohol, and yet currently there are 10.1 million underage drinkers in this nation (2002 National Household Survey on Drug Use and Health). Alcohol is a major factor in the three leading causes of death of America's teens: motor vehicle crashes, homicides and suicides. Further, underage drinking does not just harm the drinker: half of the people who die in traffic crashes involving underage drinking drivers are people other than the drinking drivers. Underage drinking is not harmless fun. There is no such thing as "responsible" underage drinking.

Progress was made in the 1980's, most notably with the raising of the minimum drinking age to 21—a law that has saved over 20,000 young lives. But we still have a national mentality that accepts underage drinking as a mere "rite of passage," and underage drinking rates remain inexcusably high and have not improved for the past decade.

According to 2002 Monitoring the Future data, nearly half (48.6 percent) of all high school seniors report drinking in the last 30 days, a much larger proportion of youth than those who report either using marijuana (21.5 percent) or smoking (26.7 percent). The proportion of high school seniors who reported drinking in the last 30 days was the same in 2002 as it was over a decade ago in 1993. Additionally, 29 percent of seniors report having five or more drinks on at least one occasion in the past two weeks, a percentage virtually unchanged since 1993.

Teens have easy access to alcohol. They are saturated with irresponsible alcohol ads. Underage drinking laws are not well enforced. And, parents and communities often look the other way when kids drink, in many cases even providing the alcohol.

We've all heard the line: "Well, at least they're not using drugs." The fact is, alcohol IS the illegal drug of choice for teens.

Consequences Associated with Youth Alcohol Use

The consequences of youth alcohol use are staggering. Research demonstrates that the younger someone starts drinking, the more likely they are to suffer from alcohol-related problems later in life, including alcohol dependence and drunk driving. Children who drink before age 15 are four times more likely to become alcohol dependent than those who delay drinking until they are 21.

More than 17,000 people are killed each year in alcohol-related crashes and approximately one-half million others are injured. In 2000, 69 percent of youth killed in alcohol-related traffic crashes involved underage drinking drivers. Although young drivers make up a mere 7 percent of the driving population, they constitute 13 percent of the alcohol-involved drivers in fatal crashes.

The 1999 National Survey of Drinking and Driving among Drivers Age 16—20 revealed that youth drove 11 million times after drinking in the past year. Their average blood alcohol level was .10 percent, three times the level of all drivers who drove after drinking. Forty percent of youth who drove after drinking had at least one passenger in the vehicle. Clearly young drivers are putting themselves and others at risk. Society has an obligation to protect motorists from the risky behavior of underage drinkers. Society also has an obligation to protect kids from themselves.

Alcohol is also implicated in a large portion of deaths and injuries caused by dangers other than drinking and driving. According to the NAS, nearly 40 percent of youth under age 21 who died from drowning, burns and falls tested positive for alcohol. Youth alcohol use is also associated with violence and suicidal behavior. Individuals under 21 commit 45 percent of rapes, 44 percent of robberies, and 37 percent of other assaults, and it is estimated that 50 percent of violent crime is alcohol-related.

Sexual violence, as well as unplanned and unprotected sexual activity, is another consequence of youth alcohol use. A 2002 National Institute on Alcohol Abuse and Alcoholism (NIAAA) study titled "A Call to Action: Changing the Culture of Drinking at U.S. Colleges" found that each year more than 70,000 students aged 18–24 are victims of alcohol-related sexual assault or date rape. Additionally, the report found that 600,000 students were assaulted by another drinking college student annually.

Groundbreaking work in the field of neuroscience sheds further light on the long-term consequences of youth alcohol use. We know that the human brain continues to develop into the early 20's. As research in this area continues to emerge, studies show that heavy alcohol use by youth has disproportionately negative effects on the physical development of the brain, and that alcohol use during adolescence has a direct negative effect on brain functioning.

In addition to the human costs associated with underage drinking, the economic cost to society is staggering. It is conservatively estimated that underage drinking costs this nation $53 billion dollars each year, including $19 billion from traffic crashes and $29 billion from violent crime. The NAS points out that this estimate is "somewhat incomplete" and "does not include medical costs other than those associated with traffic crashes" and other potential factors contributing to the social costs of underage drinking. The NAS concludes that "the $53 billion appears to be an underestimate of the social costs of underage drinking." (p. 70) As parents, as educators, as legislators, knowing that underage alcohol use has such serious consequences, we have a responsibility to treat this problem with the emphasis that it deserves. Underage drinking is not a childhood rite of passage—it is a threat to our children's health and safety, brain development, to their potential and to their futures.

National Efforts to Combat Underage Drinking Woefully Inadequate

While illicit drugs and tobacco youth prevention have received considerable attention and funding from the federal government, underage drinking has consistently been ignored. NAS confirms this:

> In fiscal 2000, the nation spent approximately $1.8 billion on preventing illicit drug use (Office of National Drug Control Policy, 2003), which was 25 times the amount, $71.1 million, targeted at preventing underage alcohol use. (p. 14)

Not only is there minimal funding available to states and local communities specifically targeted to reduce youth alcohol use, there is also no coordinated national effort to reduce and prevent underage drinking. In May 2001, the General Accounting Office (GAO) released a report outlining federal funds aimed at preventing underage drinking. The report provided concrete evidence that: 1) the federal government's approach to youth alcohol use prevention is disjointed and 2) funding for youth alcohol prevention is woefully inadequate.

GAO found that multiple federal agencies play some role in underage drinking prevention, and that only a very small portion—7 percent—of total funds available for alcohol and other drug use both had a specific focus on alcohol and identified youth or youth and the broader community as the specific target population.

Citing the GAO and additional research, the NAS report concludes the following:

> ...there is no coordinated, central mechanism for disseminating research findings or providing technical assistance to grantees or others interested in developing strategies that target underage drinking—the committee is not aware of any ongoing effort to coordinate all of the various federal efforts either within or across departments. The multitude of agencies and initiatives involved suggests the need for an interagency

> body to provide national leadership and provide a single federal voice on the issue of underage drinking. (p. 236–237)
>
> The NAS report also adds that "community efforts are most likely to succeed if they have strong and informed leadership" and that "resources are needed for training and leadership development for coalition and task force members as well as key decision makers." (p. 237–238)

MADD strongly supports NAS recommendation 12–1 which calls for the establishment of a federal interagency coordinating committee to better align federal agency efforts to prevent underage drinking. The Department of Education, working with the Department of Health and Human Services, must be a vital player in this effort.

National Adult–Oriented Media Campaign

NAS reports that education-oriented interventions should be implemented in the context of a comprehensive approach to preventing underage drinking. A focal point of this comprehensive approach is the development and implementation of a national adult-oriented media campaign that seeks to educate parents and adults about the risks associated with youth alcohol use.

MADD strongly supports NAS recommendation 6:1, which states: The federal government should fund and actively support the development of a national media effort, as a major component of an adult-oriented campaign to reduce underage drinking.

The goals of the campaign, as explained by NAS, would be to instill a broad societal commitment to reduce underage drinking, to increase specific actions by adults that are meant to discourage underage drinking, and to decrease adult conduct that facilitates underage drinking.

The need for a comprehensive public education campaign aimed at underage drinking prevention is undeniable as most parents and teens are unaware of the dangers associated with youth alcohol use. Many parents do not recognize the prevalence of or the risks associated with underage alcohol use and because of this they often facilitate their underage children's drinking by giving kids access to alcohol, by not responding to children's drinking, by not adequately monitoring their children's behavior and by not understanding the severity of the consequences of youth alcohol use. All too often, parents falsely believe that since they lived through their teen years relatively unscathed, their kids will be fine.

Seven years ago, Congress allocated $1 billion dollars to the White House Office of National Drug Control Policy (ONDCP) for an anti-drug media campaign designed to prevent youth drug use. Despite the fact that alcohol is the number one youth drug problem—both then and now—underage drinking prevention messages were excluded from the campaign. The glaring omission of alcohol from the ONDCP campaign left a gaping hole in national youth prevention efforts. America's cultural "education" on alcohol continued to rely almost entirely on irresponsible alcohol advertising, television shows and movies. A more realistic portrayal of the consequences associated with youth alcohol use is long overdue.

Since 1998, Congress has considered creating a separate media campaign to prevent underage drinking, but those attempts failed due to behind the scenes opposition from the alcohol industry. The alcohol industry instead pressured Congress to request a study as a means to delay action on a media campaign. The Congressional directive to NAS to develop a comprehensive strategy to prevent underage drinking dates back several years to repeated attempts by the public health and safety communities to establish a media campaign that addresses youth alcohol use.

When the alcohol industry learned that the NAS might recommend prevention measures it opposes, alcohol interests tried to inappropriately influence the content of the report, fault the NAS expert panel, and criticize and discredit the findings while they were being formulated. Before the NAS report was even released, the beer industry took out full-page ads in Roll Call, the Hill, Congress Daily and other Capitol Hill publications in an attempt to discredit the report findings. The beer industry complained that they did not have enough influence on the NAS report.

The alcohol industry seeks to limit underage drinking prevention efforts by pointing fingers at parents as those who must bear responsibility for educating their kids. Parents do play a vital role in youth alcohol prevention efforts, but they—along with other adults who make youth access to alcohol easy—must be educated about the risks and consequences associated with underage drinking. And, research tells us that underage drinking is much more than a "family problem." Even parents who incorporate a no-use message about alcohol are swimming upstream as their kids grow up in a world in which alcohol is easy to obtain, irresponsible alcohol advertising is omnipresent, and underage drinking laws are not well-enforced.

A national adult-oriented media campaign to prevent underage drinking is necessary to elevate this public health issue and to support effective prevention efforts at the national, state and local level. The American public needs and deserves these messages.

Increased Funding and Institutionalization Needed for Alcohol Prevention within Safe and Drug Free Schools

On January 8, 2002, President Bush signed into law the No Child Left Behind Act (NCLB) of 2001. The NCLB emphasizes the Administration's commitment to provide support for elementary and secondary education to ensure that every student achieves academic success.

But, despite the staggering impact of alcohol-related problems among students, and the clear link between youth alcohol use and school achievement, our educational system does not provide stable, targeted funding for underage drinking prevention. It is important to recognize the relationship between academic performance and youth alcohol use:

- Research indicates that adolescents who use alcohol may remember 10 percent less of what they have learned than those who don't drink. (Brown SA, Tapert SF, Granholm E,—et al., 2000. Neurocognitive functioning of adolescents: Effects of protracted alcohol use. Alcoholism: Clinical and Experimental Research. 24(2):164–171)

- Among eighth graders, higher absenteeism rates were associated with greater rates of alcohol use in the past month. (O'Malley PM, Johnston LD, Bachman JG. 1998. Alcohol use among adolescents. Alcohol Health & Research World. 22(2):85–93)
- Among eighth graders, students with higher grade point averages reported less alcohol use in the past month. (O'Malley PM, Johnston LD, Bachman JG. 1998.

Alcohol use among adolescents. Alcohol Health & Research World. 22(2):85–93) The Safe and Drug–Free Schools Program was reauthorized under NCLB and is the federal government's primary vehicle for reducing drug, alcohol, tobacco use, and violence, through education and prevention activities in the nation's schools.

This program consists of two major components: (1) State Grants for Drug and Violence Prevention Programs and (2) National Programs. State Grants is a formula grant program that provides funds to state and local education agencies, as well as governors, for a wide range of school- and community-based education and prevention activities. Communities rely on state grant funding for valuable prevention activities.

Under the Safe and Drug–Free Schools and Communities Act the term "drug" includes controlled substances, the illegal use of alcohol and tobacco, and the harmful, abusive, or addictive use of other substances, including inhalants or anabolic steroids.

Overall funding for the Department of Education's Safe and Drug–Free Schools State Grants initiative has remained at very low levels. Historically, the State Grants program is at approximately the same level of funding it received in 1990, and is currently lower than the amount it received in 1991. The Administration's fiscal year 05 budget request contains 441 million dollars for State Grants, the same level of funding enacted in fiscal year 04, and a 28 million dollar decrease from the fiscal year 03 enacted level.

Quite significantly to youth alcohol prevention advocates, the Administration's fiscal year 05 budget request proposes a 30 million dollar reduction in K–12 alcohol prevention programming. This funding represented the only amount within Safe and Drug–Free Schools that was specifically targeted to K–12 alcohol prevention.

While a very modest sum compared to the economic and social costs of youth alcohol use, this cut demonstrates a clear lack of commitment to reducing underage drinking. Our schools require a stable, dedicated funding base for youth alcohol prevention. As more schools focus on violence prevention, more and more funds continue to be directed away from youth alcohol prevention.

Within the confines of Safe and Drug–Free Schools, alcohol programs must compete with a variety of other drug and violence prevention activities. Local education authorities can access these federal funds for a laundry list of programs, including "counseling services; professional development services; programs for school personnel, students, law enforcement officials, judicial officials; implementing conflict resolution, peer mediation and mentoring programs; implementing character education programs and community service projects; acquiring and installing metal detectors and hiring security personnel." While these areas are all important, the result is that very few targeted funds are available for underage drinking prevention.

A stable, year-to-year funding base for underage drinking prevention is critical because it is not enough to simply provide program funds for one or two years and NAS also states that:

> Approaches that have been demonstrated to reduce youth alcohol use have many program elements in common. However, similar to other approaches recommended in this report, the committee believes that education-oriented interventions should be implemented in the context of a comprehensive approach. (p. 197)

This comprehensive approach, as stated by NAS and strongly supported by the public health community, includes development of a national media campaign to prevent underage drinking, alcohol advertising reform, limiting access, youth-oriented interventions, government assistance and coordination, research and evaluation, and community-based interventions, which I will discuss later in my testimony.

MADD supports the current, rigorous standards required by the Substance Abuse and Mental Health Services Administration (SAMHSA) and the Department of Education for programs seeking eligibility and acceptance into the National Registry of Effective Programs (NREP). Through this review process, prevention programs are evaluated and, if approved, placed on a list of programs that have been proven to prevent or reduce substance abuse and other related high-risk behaviors.

Alcohol-related expectancies are well-formed by age 12 (Christiansen et al., 1982; Jones et al., 2001). Prevention efforts targeting suicide, drop-out and violence, for example, have shown that the most effective prevention efforts begin in or long before the developmental period that precedes the problem. Since alcohol-related expectancies are developed in childhood, prior to actual use during adolescence, and expectancies are a key factor leading to use, prevention is most effective if it begins in the developmental period preceding adolescence–childhood–which means effective prevention messages must reach our children in elementary school.

The federal government has established a set of criteria for best practices in prevention education—with that system and the latest research in mind, MADD worked diligently to ensure the effectiveness of its elementary school program, Protecting You/Protecting Me.

As NAS states:

> ...interventions need to be multicomponent and integrated; sufficient in "dose" and follow-up; establish norms that support nonuse; stress parental monitoring and supervision; be interactive; be implemented with fidelity; include limitations in access; be institutionalized; avoid an exclusive focus on information and avoid congregating high-risk youth; and promote social and emotional skill development among elementary school students. (p. 197)

NAS continues with:

> Significant developmental changes occur during adolescence. For educational interventions to be effective, they must be delivered throughout this period—multiyear programs should be encouraged. (p. 198) Protecting You/Protecting Me is an alcohol use prevention curriculum for grades 1–5. It was created in direct response to parents and community leaders seeking a program for elementary school students that could be incorporated into the core curriculum. PY/PM was named a Model Program by the U.S. Department of Health and Human Services and can be found on the NREP list.

PY/PM includes the latest brain research, provides all curriculum and training materials necessary for national replication and includes an evaluation component, which continually demonstrates significant results. The PY/PM curriculum teaches basic safety skills, alcohol's effects on the developing brain and shows kids how to protect themselves by making good decisions, such as what to do when riding in a car with an unsafe driver. The curriculum is designed to fill the gap in current prevention programs that have not yet incorporated the latest research on children's brains and the developmental risks associated with exposure to alcohol before the age of 21.

The goal of the curriculum is to prevent youth alcohol-related death and injury, focusing on the risks of underage consumption of alcoholic beverages, and vehicle-related risks, including those associated with riding as a passenger in vehicles in which the driver is not alcohol-free.

Evaluation of PY/PM has shown that students receiving the lessons are:

- more knowledgeable about their brains
- more media literate
- less likely to ride with a driver who is not alcohol-free
- less likely to drink when they are teenagers

PY/PM is endorsed by the American Academy of Pediatrics and the National Association of Elementary School Principals. By the end of 2003, nearly 200,000 elementary students were exposed to MADD's PY/PM's lessons in over 1,200 schools across the country. MADD is committed to continued growth of this program as we seek to create a culture where underage drinking is not a "rite of passage."

Program Implementation

As NAS points out, "identifying and selecting model programs are only part of the process in launching a successful education strategy." (p. 201) Local communities and education authorities have a wide range of choices when designing their prevention plans and selecting programs. Once identified however, many good programs do not have the capacity or willingness to provide the necessary technical assistance to ensure effectiveness at the local level. In fact, NAS finds that:

> Experience over the past two decades reveals that most schools do not implement research-based programs as intended or do not continue to use them over time. Failure to institutionalize interventions is likely to prevent them from realizing their full potential. Federal and state policies are needed to encourage and support the institutionalization of research-based programs. (p. 210)

Often program developers will not alter their programs or work with local educators and communities on implementation issues. This lack of attention to local communities can significantly lessen the impact of prevention programs. Model Programs are thoroughly tested and evaluated in order to be effective; however when the fidelity of the programs is not protected during implementation, it is impossible to ensure the programs will achieve their desired results. While the DOE requires the use of research-based programs, more needs to be done to ensure that programs are implemented the way in which they were intended.

MADD urges the committee to support funding for program developers to ensure that prevention programs have the necessary infrastructure to provide technical support to communities. The federal government must make a commitment to local school teachers, principals, counselors and parents to reject an ivory tower approach to prevention programming by ensuring that trained professionals will be there to roll up their sleeves and help local schools use Model Programs in the most effective way.

Increased Emphasis/Funding Needed for Prevention Research As stated earlier, it is absolutely essential that Model Programs be rigorously evaluated and identified through the NREP process; however maintaining the efficacy of a Model Program goes far beyond the initial award. There must be a long-term commitment to continually re-evaluate prevention programs and make certain that they remain relevant. MADD and many other prevention groups have been able to identify funding to develop and initially evaluate programs to meet the initial requirements of the NREP review process. But the pursuit of ongoing, long-term evaluation requires an increased financial commitment.

NAS supports this:

> Both SAMHSA and the Department of Education have demonstrated a commitment to funding research based interventions. The committee believes that this interest, and the effectiveness of funded programs, would be enhanced by a standard evaluation expectation across all funded programs.

Programs also need to be provided with tools for conducting research and evaluation." (p. 247)

MADD strongly supports NAS recommendation 12–9:

> States and the federal government—particularly the U.S. Department of Health and Human Services and the U.S. Department of Education—should fund the development and evaluation of programs to cover all underage populations.

MADD urges the committee to seek increased funding levels to specifically support longitudinal research to ensure the ongoing effectiveness of Model Programs.

To guarantee that our children continue to receive the best that prevention has to offer, the federal government must commit time, resources and attention to the long term assessment of all Model Programs. This is a measure that will protect investments made by the federal government and ensure that taxpayer dollars are being spent on programs that work year after year.

Community–Based Interventions

As stated earlier in recommendation 10:2 and throughout the report, NAS outlines the need for community-based interventions as part of a comprehensive underage drinking prevention strategy. School-based interventions will have only modest results if they are not coupled with proven, research-based community interventions. That is why MADD designed Youth In Action (YIA). YIA is a community-based prevention approach that utilizes effective environmental strategies such as limiting availability of alcohol to minors, creating partnerships with law enforcement and working to change alcohol policies. Young people work on specific community projects which are proven to significantly reduce the availability of alcohol for teens and raise compliance with related 21 Minimum Drinking Age Laws. Such practices have been found to be highly effective and are substantiated by numerous studies cited in the Pacific Institute for Research and Evaluation report, "Regulatory Strategies for Preventing Youth Access to Alcohol: Best Practices."

YIA teams have been trained in more than 40 communities across the country.

Their partnerships with local law enforcement agencies, schools and community leaders have helped pass key underage drinking legislation and encourage enforcement of laws that have saved young lives. Youth In Action focuses on the community environment that condones underage drinking: from the store clerk who doesn't check IDs, to the police officer who might pour out the alcohol and send teens home, to the adult who doesn't mind buying beer for a kid who slips him or her an extra $10. YIA teams look for community solutions to underage drinking to work in concert with many of the school-based interventions already in place in their communities.

Youth In Action teams engage in very specific interventions because research says these projects work. For example, YIA teams conduct Alcohol Purchase Surveys, where a young looking 21 year old attempts to purchase alcohol without an ID. No actual purchase is made. It is merely a community survey conducted to determine whether retail clerks would have sold alcohol to a presumed minor without ID.

In the Greater Boston area, MADD's Youth In Action team began doing Alcohol Purchase Surveys in 2000. At that time only 64 percent of surveyed stores carded the legal age buyer. After concentrated efforts with local law enforcement these numbers increased to 81 percent of buyers being carded by 2002.

YIA teams also conduct Shoulder–Tap Surveys. During these surveys, local police observe the youth for safety purposes as they approach adults outside an alcohol retailer and ask if these adults would willingly purchase alcohol for them because they are too young to legally buy.

That same YIA team I mentioned from Boston also conducted Shoulder Taps in 2001. Students approached 100 people at 15 different package stores. The good news is they found that 83 people would not purchase alcohol for them. The disheartening news is that they also determined that they only needed to be out for an average of 15 minutes before they could find a complete stranger willing to say yes.

Instead of money, the adults who agreed to purchase alcohol were given a card outlining Massachusetts state law and listing the penalty for furnishing alcohol to a minor. Those who refused to purchase alcohol were handed a card thanking them for serving their community by refusing to provide alcohol to a minor.

Students involved with Youth In Action also conduct two projects in support of law enforcement. Many organize Law Enforcement Recognition Events where teens publicly thank local law enforcement officials who are working to prevent underage drinking and impaired driving. These events range from formal banquets, to media events, to YIA teams dropping off snacks for officers at the station or out on location where police officers are working on the job.

The second project with police involves students preparing "Roll Call Briefings."

YIA teams ask to present to police officers during their shift change meetings when officers are beginning their shifts. Two or three YIA members go to the police station with an adult leader to encourage police officers to enforce the Zero Tolerance Laws that make it illegal for youth to drive after drinking. Many YIA teams hand out printed cards or notepads that outline the law and declare the teens support for the police officers in enforcing the law.

The inclusion of tested community-based programs that engage students in underage drinking prevention as part of a comprehensive strategy is vital. MADD urges the committee to pursue action to allow community-based programs to be accepted as Model Programs. Young people must not only learn about alcohol in the classroom but must be engaged in solutions through learning opportunities that support a multi-component, integrated prevention plan.

Alcohol–Industry Efforts

MADD continues to push for evaluation efforts and proven programs because without hard data we do not know what types of messages will work. Unevaluated programs may be useless or, worse, counterproductive. As the NAS states, "interventions that rely solely on provision of information alone, fear tactics, or messages about not drinking until one is "old enough" have consistently been found to be ineffective in reducing alcohol use, and in some cases, produce boomerang effects." (p. 195)

This is why many in the public health community remain highly skeptical of the value of the alcohol industry's underage drinking programs. By and large, the alcohol industry has relied on unproven messages and tactics to combat underage drinking. The NAS reports that it "is aware of only one industry-sponsored education program that has been independently evaluated," (p. 195) and further research was suggested on that particular program.

The alcohol industry charged that the NAS panel did not review industry funded programs, but this could not be farther from the truth. The NAS reviewed all of the materials submitted, but found that the industry's material had no backing in science. This led NAS to report:

> "Based on our own review of the materials submitted by industry representatives, the alcohol prevention literature, and the other materials and testimony submitted to the committee, we believe that industry efforts to prevent and reduce underage drinking, however sincere, should be redirected and strengthened." (p. 132)

NAS went on to rearticulate the need for strong scientific evidence to support any underage drinking program:

> ...industry-funded messages and programs should be delivered directly to young people only if they rest on a scientific foundation, as judged by qualified, independent organizations, or incorporate rigorous evaluation. Programs that have an exclusive focus on providing information have been demonstrated to be ineffective at reducing alcohol use and should be avoid-ed. (p. 134)

Quite significantly, a typical industry-funded "responsibility" ad is branded with the alcohol company name, which leads many public health experts to conclude that "responsibility" ads are simply another means to promote brand recognition and loyalty.

A recent study by the Center on Alcohol Marketing and Youth (CAMY 2003) reported that in 2001 the alcohol industry spent $23.2 million dollars to air 2,379 "responsibility" messages, while in contrast the industry spent $812.2 million on 208,909 product advertisements. There were 179 product ads for every ad that referred to the legal drinking age.

NAS reports that:

> In 2001, alcoholic beverage companies spent $1.6 billion on advertising and print media, broadcast media, billboards, and other venues—known as measured media purchases. At least twice that amount was spent on unmeasured promotion, which includes sponsorships, product placement payment in entertainment media, point-of-sale

advertising, discount promotion, apparel and other items with brand-name logos, and other activities (Federal Trade Commission, 1999). (p. 134)

The market certainly rewards those manufacturers that can tap the youth market. The NAS reports that underage drinkers consumed anywhere from 10 to 20 percent of all alcohol consumed in 2000, representing somewhere between 11 to 22 billion dollars. Beer is overwhelmingly the most common alcoholic drink consumed by underage drinkers.

Now "malternatives" or "alcopops" have climbed onto the advertising bandwagon to capture more of the youth market (such as Smirnoff Ice, Bacardi Silver, and Skyy Blue). MADD is deeply concerned with the growing number of ads for liquor-branded, malt-based beverages that have a flavor and marketing plan that appeals to our kids. Just like beer, the distilled spirits industry is being given a "free pass" to establish brand recognition and loyalty among youth. NAS states that: A particularly troubling illustration of the youth-specific attractions of an alcohol marketing campaign concerns so-called "alcopops," sweet, flavored alcoholic malt beverages. Recent survey data suggest that these products are more popular with teenagers than with adults, both in terms of awareness and use. (p. 135)

New data from the 2003 Monitoring the Futures Survey confirms that these drinks are popular with teens: nearly 80 percent of high school seniors who drink had consumed an alcohol-pop within the past year.

Additionally, despite the alcohol industry's claims, CAMY reports that young people under 21 are reached at a higher proportion to their numbers in the population by print alcohol ads. Our youth see far more beer, distilled spirits and malternative advertising in magazines than adults. In 2001 alone, nearly one-third of all measured magazine alcohol ads were placed in 10 publications with a youth audience of 25 percent or more.

NAS points out that the dispute over whether alcohol advertising "causes" underage drinking is simply an "unnecessary distraction" from the most important task at hand: the alcohol industry must do a better job of refraining from marketing products or engaging in promotional activities that appeal to youth. NAS concludes that if the industry fails to respond in a meaningful way to this challenge, the case for government action becomes compelling. Although beer is the favorite alcoholic beverage among young people, the beer industry has advertised for years with little or no restrictions or standards from the networks. Strong alcohol advertising restrictions must be mandatory for all segments of the alcohol industry—including ads for beer, wine, liquor and malt-based beverages.

It is odd that an industry that studies and hones its marketing messages so well has no data on the effectiveness of its underage drinking programs. At best, the industry is inept in this area; at worst, they are a malevolent force.

In no other context would we trust that a product manufacturer would aggressively work to convince a segment of the population not to buy their products. Yet in regards to underage drinking, we are willing to trust the health, well-being and education of our children in large part to the care of the alcohol industry.

The government must act to make sure that science-based, effective programs are not lost in the din of advertising and industry messages. If the alcohol industry can create programs that stand up to scientific scrutiny, then we can reexamine this; in the meantime, it is past time for action.

Conclusion

Armed with the knowledge that underage alcohol use results in significant negative social and economic consequences, including irreversible damage to the adolescent brain, our nation can no longer pretend that underage drinking is a rite of passage. Our children deserve more. It is time to face the sobering reality that if we do not put an end to the complacent attitude about underage drinking, we continue to put our children in harm's way.

More youth drink alcohol than smoke tobacco or use other illegal drugs, yet federal investments in preventing underage drinking pale in comparison with resources targeted at preventing illicit drug use. The media constantly reports on the countless numbers of alcohol-related deaths and injuries of today's youth, but our nation accepts and even enables these preventable tragedies. The future of our nation's youth continues to hang in the balance. Underage drinking is illegal, and yet millions of kids continue to engage in this high-risk behavior every month, every week-end, and even every day.

The NAS has reviewed the research and has recommended strategies that will significantly reduce and prevent underage drinking. As a parent and an activist who has experienced devastating alcohol-related consequences, I urge this Committee to use the NAS recommendations as a roadmap to create a healthier future for America's youth and embrace the role you can play in expanding youth and community interventions through our nation's educational system. Thank you.

Mr. Osborne. Thank you, Mrs. Hamilton.

Ms. Hackett.

STATEMENT OF JACQUELINE HACKETT, STUDENT LEADERSHIP COUNCIL, STUDENTS AGAINST DESTRUCTIVE DECISIONS

Ms. Hackett. Mr. Chairman, members of the Subcommittee and distinguished panelists, my name is Jacqueline Hackett, and I am a senior at Souderton Area High School in Montgomery County, Pennsylvania.

I have been actively involved in Students Against Destructive Decisions since I was in the eighth grade, first at the local level and now nationally, where I serve as an executive committee member for the SADD Student Leadership Council.

As a high school student, I am very aware of the lifestyle and the activities chosen by some of my peers. Friday night parties are not kept secret, nor is anyone left unaware of what happens at these events. The reality of high school life is that underage drinking is a very big deal and a serious problem that affects not only those who choose to use but also others in the high school community and ultimately my entire generation.

Let me tell you a little bit about SADD and how it works. Since being founded in 1981 as Students Against Drunk Driving, SADD has been committed to empowering young people to say no to alcohol and other drugs and encouraging young people to serve as role models in their own communities.

In 1997 in response to young people themselves, SADD expanded its name and its mission and now sponsors chapters called Students Against Destructive Decisions. SADD continues to endorse and affirm a no use message related to the use of alcohol and other drugs. With this expanded focus, SADD now highlights prevention in all destructive behaviors and attitudes that are harmful to youth, focusing particularly on underage drinking, substance abuse, impaired driving, teen violence, suicide and depression.

Currently there are 10,000 SADD chapters in middle schools, high schools and colleges around the United States with 350,000 active members and seven million students in the schools where SADD chapters exist. Over the past 23 years, literally millions of people have gone through the SADD program, proving that SADD serves a necessary role and delivers a strong and unwavering message.

The efforts of SADD have been proven to work. An independent study conducted in the late '90's showed that students in schools with an established SADD chapter are more aware of and informed about the risks of underage drinking, other drug use and impaired driving.

Students in schools with a SADD chapter are also more likely to hold attitudes reflecting positive reasons not to use alcohol. Alcohol is the No. 1 drug of choice among our nation's youth.

I won't repeat all the statistics because I am sure you know them, but here is just one. In 2002 there were more than 2,400 alcohol-related traffic deaths among students 15 to 20 years old, more than 200 teen lives lost each month to impaired driving alone. Across the country, SADD is working to respond to this pervasive youth epidemic. Perhaps the most important reason that SADD works is because it's students who talk to each other, using words and activities that are more likely to make a difference.

After all, young people are the ones who are actually drinking the beers, putting the keys into the ignition and piling into a car with friends who have been drinking in the driver's seat.

SADD chapters provide information and education about the harmful effects of drugs and alcohol, but they also host alternative drug-free activities for students, mentor younger elementary and middle school students, and reach out to other groups in the community, such as law enforcement, the media, and the business community. My chapter has held prom graduation programs, offered dances as drug-free alternative events, and co-hosted a picnic with the local YMCA.

SADD offers a safe haven for those who have made the conscious decision not to use. SADD students become alternative role models and consciously work to bring people together who believe in the no use message for youth and want to make a positive difference in their community.

All the individual SADD chapters working together have a huge potential to present positive change in their communities. We need support though. We need more people to acknowledge our efforts and provide us with the resources to implement effective programming.

If in my state the Pennsylvania Department of Education were to embrace the 550 Pennsylvania SADD chapters working on prevention efforts at the local level, link them with community coalitions and local law enforcement initiatives and provide coordinating services that magnify the energy and drive of fellow SADD students working within every school, there would indeed be a strong statewide movement opposing the destructive influences of alcohol on our youth.

With the state support not only in Pennsylvania but in every state in the country, SADD would be able to spread its message even further, implement effective prevention programming within the schools and ultimately change behaviors and attitudes of the youth across the United States.

The underage drinking epidemic needs a strong movement against it to challenge the negative and risky attitudes of young people and SADD is that movement.

SADD students are the troops and they are ready for the country, they are ready for the country to support them so that they can win this war.

Thank you very much for giving me this opportunity to speak today with you about this very serious problem that I am committed to addressing through my work in SADD. Underage drinking is dangerous and often deadly and I urge you to rally behind students like myself and give us the support we need to continue the work that we are doing every day in our communities. SADD is a force that needs your collaboration and support.

[The prepared statement of Ms. Hackett follows:]

Statement of Jacqueline Hackett, Student Leadership Council, Students against Destructive Decisions

Mr. Chairman, Members of the Subcommittee, Distinguished Panelists: My name is Jacqueline Hackett and I am a senior at Souderton Area High School in Montgomery County, Pennsylvania. I've been actively involved in Students against Destructive Decisions since I was in eighth grade; first at the local level and now nationally where I serve on the executive committee of the SADD Student Leadership Council.

As a high school student, I'm very aware of the lifestyle and activities chosen by some of my peers. Friday night parties aren't kept secret, nor is anyone left unaware of what happens at these events. The reality of high school life is that underage drinking is a very big deal and a serious problem that affects not only those who choose to use, but also others in the high school community and ultimately my entire generation.

Let me tell you a little bit about what SADD is and how it works. Since being founded in 1981 as Students against Driving Drunk, SADD has been committed to empowering young people to "say no" to alcohol and other drugs, and encouraging young people to serve as role models in their communities. In 1997, in response to young people themselves, SADD expanded its mission and name, and now sponsors chapters called Students Against Destructive Decisions. SADD continues to endorse a firm "no use" message related to use of alcohol and other drugs. With its expanded focus, SADD now highlights prevention of all destructive behaviors and attitudes that are harmful to youth, focusing particularly on underage drinking, substance abuse, impaired driving, teen violence, suicide and depression.

Currently there are 10,000 SADD chapters in middle schools, high schools, and colleges around the United States with 350,000 active members and seven million students in the schools where SADD exists. Over the past 23 years, literally millions of people have gone through the SADD program, proving that SADD serves a necessary role and delivers a strong and unwavering message.

The efforts of SADD have been proven to work. An independent study conducted in the late 1990s showed that students in schools with an established SADD chapter are more aware of and informed about the risks of underage drinking, other drug use, and impaired driving. Students in schools with a SADD chapter are also more likely to hold attitudes reflecting positive reasons not to use alcohol.

Alcohol is the number one drug of choice among our nation's youth. I won't repeat all the statistics because I'm sure you know them, but here is just one. In 2002, there were more than 2,400 alcohol-related traffic deaths among 15 to 20 year olds, more than 200 teen lives lost each month to impaired driving alone.

Across the country, SADD is working to respond to this pervasive youth epidemic.

Perhaps the most important reason that SADD works is that it's about students talking to each other, using words and activities that are most likely to make a difference. After all, young people are the ones who actually drink the beer, put the key in the ignition or pile into a car with a friend who has been drinking in the driver's seat.

SADD chapters provide information and education about the harmful effects of drugs and alcohol, but they also host alternative drug-free activities for students, mentor younger elementary and middle school students and reach out to other groups in the community such as law enforcement, the media and the business community. My chapter has held prom and graduation programs, offered dances as drug-free alternative events, and co-hosted a picnic with the local YMCA. SADD chapters offer a "safe haven" for those who have made the conscientious decision not to use. SADD students become alternative role models and continuously work to bring people together who believe in the "no use" message for youth and want to make a positive difference in their community.

All of the individual SADD chapters working together have a huge potential to present positive change in their communities. We need support though. We need more people to acknowledge our efforts and provide us with resources to implement effective programming. If in my state, the Pennsylvania Department of Education were to embrace the 550 Pennsylvania SADD chapters working on prevention efforts at the local level, link them with community coalitions and local law enforcement initiatives, and provide coordination services that magnified the energy and drive of fellow SADD students working within every school, there would indeed be a strong state-wide movement opposing the destructive influence of alcohol on our youth. With state support, not only in Pennsylvania but in every state in the country, SADD would be able to spread the message even further, implement effective prevention programming within the schools, and ultimately change behaviors and attitudes of youth across the United States. The underage drinking epidemic needs a strong oppositional movement to challenge the negative and risky attitudes of young people, and SADD is that movement. SADD students are the troops and they're ready for the country to support them so they can win this war.

Thank you very much for giving me the opportunity to speak with you today about this very serious problem that I am committed to addressing through my work with SADD. Underage drinking is dangerous and often deadly, and I urge you to rally behind students like myself and give us the support we need to continue the work we are doing every day in our communities. SADD is a force that needs your collaboration and support.

Mr. Osborne. Thank you very much.

Mrs. Katz.

Statement of Francine I. Katz, Vice President, Corporate Communications, Anheuser-Busch Companies, Inc.

Mrs. KATZ. Good morning, Mr. Vice Chairman and distinguished members of the Subcommittee. My name is Francine Katz, and for 14 years I have headed a department at Anheuser-Busch of over 20 people working to fight alcohol abuse, including underage drinking. I am pleased to be sharing the floor today with others who share a commitment to this issue.

I hope you will remember three things from what I have to say.

First, that the more than 830,000 people who brew, package, distribute, and sell America's beers care about this issue and want to be part of the solution. Personally, I feel passionately about this issue, not just because of my job at Anheuser-Busch but because I am a mother. I have a 17-year-old daughter and a 12-year-old son, and I care about this issue just like every other mom out there.

The second thing I would ask you to remember is that the best way to fight underage drinking is through education and awareness, starting early and in the home.

Third, things are getting better. There is much more work to be done, but our nation has made some real progress in this fight.

Our industry is committed to addressing underage drinking and we want to be part of the solution and at Anheuser-Busch we take great pride in the beers we brew, but we also understand the responsibility that accompanies selling an adult product.

People in our industry come from all walks of life. They are brewers and bottlers, wholesalers and retailers. They are waiters, they are MBAs and they are secretaries. They are salespeople and they are union workers. They are churchgoers and PTA members.

They live all over the United States. They are moms. They are dads. And they all share a commitment to fighting underage drinking.

We believe the best way to address this issue is through education and awareness and in this regard we take a three-prong approach.

First and foremost, our efforts are directed at parents, to help them address this issue with their kids. Why? Because every year for the last decade in a national poll of youth conducted by the Roper research organization youths themselves have identified their parents' far and away as the most important factor in their decisions to drink or refrain from drinking.

Our efforts on this front involve several programs. The first is called "Family Talk About Drinking," which is a guide book that's available in five languages and helps parents of children as young as 8 years old begin the conversation with their children and carry it through their teenage years. We've given out over 5 million copies of this program since it was introduced in 1990.

The second program is called "College Talk," and it's a program for those parents whose teens are heading off to college, and the goal of that program is to help parents help their teens continue to make responsible decisions in their college years. But we also recognize that some youth don't get the kind of parental influence that they need at home, and we have been a strong supporter of mentoring initiatives designed to help adults who are caring adults make a difference in the lives of youth who need that kind of positive influence.

The second prong of our efforts is aimed at retailers. Because we don't actually sell our products to the public, but rather we sell to wholesalers who in turn sell to retailers, and those retailers sell to the public. So we focus on efforts on those retailers who are on the front line, and we give them training and tools to spot fake IDs and stop sales to minors. And the nation's largest retailers, including 7-11, Circle K, Safeway and Publics join us in this effort.

I'd like to show the Subcommittee a commercial which debuted on last year's Academy Awards and aired again this month on the Super Bowl which emphasizes the powerful role that retailers can play in this fight.

[Videotape is played.]

Mrs. KATZ. The third prong of efforts involves programs aimed at young people. The most visible example is a speaker's bureau, comprised of third parties who bring messages into schools through live presentations. These speakers cover topics such as drunk driving, alcohol poisoning, building refusal skills, and enhancing self-esteem. Over the last 5 years, they've reached more than 1.4 million students.

Each of these programs emphasizes that there is no excuse for breaking the law, and that youth must understand that such behavior will have consequences.

Mr. Vice Chairman, members of the Subcommittee, over the last 22 years, Anheuser-Busch and its family of wholesalers across the country have invested nearly half a billion dollars in these efforts.

But equally important to this financial investment is the human capital that we and our wholesalers have expended in this fight.

Whether it's manning a booth to hand out Family Talk about drinking to parents or hosting training sessions for servers to help them spot fake IDs, meeting with school principals to offer a third-party speaker for students, this human capital demonstrates our collective commitment to being part of the solution.

Finally, it is important to acknowledge that progress has been made on this front so that parents know their efforts are working, so that retailers know checking IDs is working, and so that teens know that most of their peers are making the good decision not to drink, because many are. According to the U.S. Department of Health and Human Services, 82 percent of today's teens do not drink. The University of Michigan's Monitoring the Future Survey sponsored by the National Institute on Drug Abuse reports that the percentage of high school seniors having a drink in the last 30 days has declined 32 percent since 1982.

I realize that Mrs. Hamilton also cited the same statistic. However, her data is from 2002, not the most recent 2003 report, which was released 2 months ago, and shows that this figure is at a record low level.

And according to the U.S. Department of Transportation, teen drunk driving fatalities have declined 61 percent since 1982. A large part of the credit for this progress goes to groups like Mothers Against Drunk Driving and SADD. And while we've made significant progress, this battle is far from over.

In closing, let me say that the commitment I've spoken of today is shared by my colleagues at Miller, Coors, Heineken, and other brewers. We believe that the best way to continue the progress made in this fight against underage drinking is through education, especially involving parents, and the collective investment we make in our youth today will ensure their safe passage into adulthood.

Thank you.

[The prepared statement of Mrs. Katz follows:]

Testimony of: Francine Katz, Vice President, Corporate Communications, Anheuser–Busch Companies, Inc.

Good morning, Mr. Chairman, Mr. Vice Chairman and distinguished members of the Subcommittee. My name is Francine Katz, and I'm the vice president responsible for Anheuser–Busch's longstanding efforts to fight alcohol abuse, an area I have been working in since 1990. I also am the mother of a 17-year-old daughter and a 12-year-old son, so I am dealing with these issues as a parent, too.

I thank you for the opportunity to be here to address a topic that is important to all of us at Anheuser–Busch and to our fellow brewers. I hope that you remember three things from my statement here today: First, that the men and women who brew, package, distribute and sell America's beers care about this issue and want to be part of the solution. The more than 830,000 people in this industry come from all walks of life. They are brewers and bottlers, wholesalers and waiters. They are MBAs and secretaries, sales people and union workers. They are churchgoers and members of their local PTAs. They are east coasters, west coasters and Midwesterners. They are men and women, moms and dads. And they have an important role in helping to resolve this problem. Second that our nation truly has made some significant progress in the fight against underage drinking. And third, that education, starting early and in the home, is the best way to continue that progress.

Those of us in the beer industry are also in the hospitality business. Our beers are intended to be a refreshing accompaniment to social occasions or a simple reward after a long day's work. We take great pride in being part of an industry that has had its roots in America since colonial times. We also understand the responsibility that goes along with making and marketing an adult product, and we have been at the forefront of efforts to fight the abuse of our products. I am proud to tell you that my company has invested nearly a half billion dollars thus far in these efforts, and we are committed to continuing these initiatives. And I speak for other members of our nation's beer industry. While we compete with each other as fiercely as any industry in America, in this we are united: we don't want kids to drink, and we are committed to giving parents and others who deal with the problem real solutions.

In addition to our company's efforts, each of Anheuser–Busch's independently owned beer wholesalers conduct alcohol awareness programs in their communities.

These wholesalers have an individual within their organizations with responsibility for developing an alcohol awareness activities market plan and directing their local efforts. They do this by providing our educational materials to the public, making our alcohol awareness programs part of their promotions, and purchasing print, outdoor, radio and TV awareness ads. Equally important to this financial investment is the human capital that Anheuser–Busch and our wholesalers have expended in this fight. Whether it's manning a booth to hand out materials designed to help parents talk to their kids about drinking; hosting training sessions for servers to help them spot fake IDs; meeting with school principals to offer third party speakers who address topics with students like drunk driving and alcohol awareness, this human capital demonstrates our collective commitment to being part of the solution.

We believe we have far more in common with the other witnesses on the panel than may appear at first blush. We all agree that underage drinking is a serious issue that we must aggressively fight. And I hope that we can channel our energies and resources toward this collective goal and find ways to work together in this fight.

We believe the most effective way to fight underage drinking is to use a three-prong approach, and the cornerstone of that approach is focused on parents. Don Elium, a family and child counselor, recently wrote a book called, "Raising a Teenager." In his book, Elium says that the teenage years are like a second birth of sorts, and that teens need just as much time and attention at that stage of their lives as they did when they were born. Elium goes on to say, "One of the biggest mistakes parents make is letting them make decisions they have no business making...a family is not a democracy, it is a benevolent dictatorship." As a mother myself, I know that to be true.

And despite what we may all think, youth themselves also favor strong parental involvement. According to the Roper Research Organization's Youth Poll, a nationally representative survey, 73% of youth ages 8-17 cite their parents, far and away, as the most influential factor in their decision to drink or refrain from drinking.

This poll has been conducted for over a decade, and every year, youth have overwhelmingly identified their parents as the number one influence in this decision.

Accordingly, we have invested a significant amount of our efforts in programs for parents. One such program, a guide book and video for parents called "Family Talk About Drinking," was created by an advisory panel of authorities from the areas of family counseling, alcohol treatment and education. It is available in five languages. We promote this free program through advertising and on our website, but over the years, we have also worked in partnership with groups and organizations across the country to get these materials into the hands of parents. For instance, we have worked with the attorneys general from various states to send these materials to parents. Working with the Association of Junior Leagues International, we have distributed "Family Talk" via the group's local chapters through our network of 600 wholesalers throughout the country. And for parents of teens heading off to college, we have a program called "College Talk," created by a group of authorities in the fields of student life, alcohol treatment and peer education. This program helps parents prepare their teens for responsible decision-making in college. "College Talk" is endorsed by the National Association of State Universities and Land Grant Colleges, the American Association of State Colleges and Universities, the Social Norms Resource Center and the BACCHUS and GAMMA Peer Education Network.

The second prong to our efforts to fight underage drinking is aimed at the retail level, the point-of-purchase. Under the laws governing the sale and distribution of beer, we do not sell our products to consumers. Rather, we sell to our wholesalers, they sell to retailers and retailers sell to the public. As a result, retailers are on the front lines and they play a vital role in stopping underage drinking. In cooperation with police departments, county sheriffs, and other state and local agencies, we have worked aggressively to help retailers and servers stop sales to minors. We provide materials in English, Spanish, Korean and Vietnamese for retailers to teach them how to properly check IDs and to spot fake IDs. We also disseminate "WE ID" and other point-of-sale materials that remind customers that the establishment will ask for proper identification. Among the myriad of tools we provide retailers are such things as drivers' license booklets that show valid licenses from all 50 states and serve as a useful tool for retailers—especially in college communities—who are confronted with IDs from all over the country. We have worked closely in these efforts with a number of major national retailers including 7–Eleven Stores, Circle K, Publix and Safeway Markets to put these materials to work in their stores. Our efforts in this regard were just featured in one of our Super Bowl commercials earlier this month, in which an attentive clerk deterred two teens in their attempt to buy beer.

We have also been a sponsor of several server-training programs, designed again to ensure the responsible sale and service of our products. These include Training in Intervention Procedures for servers of alcohol, or TIPs, a program developed by Dr. Morris Chafetz, founding director of the NIAAA. TIPs provides techniques for servers to avoid over serving and drunk driving situations and to ensure proper ID checking procedures.

Similar training is also presented in the BarCode and Learn2Serve programs that we support.

Over the last decade, we have also joined with our colleagues at Miller and Coors through the Beer Institute and with the National Highway Traffic Safety Administration, Major League Baseball, and other professional sports leagues in a program called "TEAM" (which stands for "Techniques for Effective Alcohol Management") to address underage drinking and abusive consumption at games and other major outdoor events. Through this partnership, we helped train all the staff at the 28 Major League Baseball stadiums in alcohol management techniques before opening day last year.

Finally, the third prong of our approach involves directing efforts at young people, to help them make good decisions. The most visible example of these efforts is a Speakers Bureau comprised of third parties from many walks of life who take their messages directly into schools. The members of the Anheuser–Busch Consumer Awareness and Education Speakers Bureau bring a message of responsibility and respect for the law to middle school and high school students around the country.

With the support of our local wholesalers, over the past five years, these speakers have reached more than 1.4 million students via 4,700 presentations throughout the country. The speakers include:

- Barbara Babb, a former critical-care flight nurse, who delivers a graphic, factual and memorable presentation on video to high school and college students about the tragic consequences of underage drinking and drunk driving.
- Michael Chatman, who shares his message of self-empowerment and personal responsibility with students across the country. The son of an abusive father, Michael grew up in Miami, joined a gang and endured the trials of life on the wrong side of the law. Finally, following a series of life-altering events, he decided to transform his life. Today, Michael has reached more than one million teenagers, helping them realize that despite negative peer pressure,

and the many other challenges they may face, underage drinking is not the answer.

- Dr. Lonnie Carton, a nationally recognized educator and family counselor, and host of the nationally syndicated radio program "Take a Minute for the Family."

Lonnie presents "Stepping Into Adolescence" a program for parents of middle-school children designed to help parents maintain open communication with their children during the middle-school years and throughout adolescence.

- Bob Anastas, the founder and former executive director of Students Against Driving Drunk (SADD), delivers a powerful presentation to high school and college students. Motivational in spirit, the program offers parents and students a timely message on how young people can build key life skills and make responsible decisions about the challenges they face. The program is also available on video.
- Emergency-room nurse Linda Dutil delivers a presentation, designed for middle-and high school students, about the real-world consequences that come from making poor choices about alcohol and drugs. Linda also teaches effective skills for resisting peer pressure and for making smart, responsible choices.
- Jason Barber tells the story of several teens, including his brother, each of who were drunk driving crash victims. What students learn during Jason's powerful presentation is that he was the intoxicated driver responsible for his brother's death. Jason was seriously injured and served prison time for vehicular man-slaughter.
- Carolyn Cornelison, who holds a Ph.D. from Florida State University where she worked as director of the Campus Alcohol and Drug Information Center for four years while advising both BACCHUS & GAMMA, delivers a program called "Courage to Care," which focuses on college drinking, taking responsibility, recognizing abuse and helping those with alcohol problems. A

member of a sorority and a former collegiate student-athlete, Carolyn has taken her "Courage to Care" message to more than 350 college campuses and has been a part of numerous Greek education, athletic department and general campus health programs.

- The "Street Smart" program, taught by certified firefighter/ paramedics, reminds students of the dangers of teen drinking, drunk driving, illegal drug use and not wearing seat belts. The program is available for presentation in English or Spanish, and uses factual information, actual medical equipment and demonstrations involving students to help them better understand the consequences of their actions. "Street Smart" is presented by members of "Stay Alive From Education" (S.A.F.E.), a non-profit organization created by firefighter/paramedics in Miami–Dade County, Florida, dedicated to reducing teen injuries and fatalities.

One of the things that each of these programs emphasizes is that there is no excuse for breaking the law—and youth must understand that such behavior will have consequences. While they are teens, our young people should not be led to believe that they are excused from acting responsibly and abiding by the law. They are expected to act with responsibility.

At the college level, we have supported campus programs that focus student attention on education and awareness, emphasizing personal responsibility and respect for the law—which means not drinking if you are under 21, and drinking responsibly if you are above the legal drinking age and choose to drink. These programs include, among others, unrestricted grants to colleges such as the University of Virginia, Florida State University, Georgetown University, Michigan State University and Virginia Commonwealth University to establish social norms programs, a positive approach that reminds college students that the large majority of their peers make healthy and responsible decisions about drinking. We have also worked closely for over three years with the National Association of State Universities and Land Grant Colleges, an organization representing more than 200 of America's largest institutions, to promote social norms and encourage responsible behavior among college students. A recent comprehensive report issued by the National Institute on Alcohol Abuse and Alcoholism (NIAAA) categorized social norms and other approaches supported by the industry as effective or promising.[11]

I mentioned earlier that it was important to cite the progress that has been made on this front—to let parents know their efforts are working, and to salute those teens who are making the right decisions. And many are. Teen drinking and teen drunk-driving fatalities have declined significantly over the last two decades. According to the U.S. Department of Health and Human Services, 82% of today's adolescents do not drink.[12] That means nearly 20 million adolescents are doing the right thing by not drinking.[13] Similarly, according to the University of Michigan survey called "Monitoring the Future," sponsored by the National Institute on Drug Abuse, the percentage of high school seniors who report having a drink in the last 30 days was 32% lower in 2002 than it was in 1982.[14] In 2003, there were nearly 410,000 fewer high school seniors who reported past-month drinking than did in 1982.[15] And beer consumption by college freshmen fell 39% in the same time frame according to the American Council on Education and researchers at the University of California at Los Angeles.[16] The latter two measurements are record lows.

In addition, the United States Department of Transportation reports that fatalities in crashes involving drunk drivers aged 16 to 20 have fallen 61% between 1982 and 2002. There were 2,500 fewer teen drunk-driving fatalities in 2002 than there were in 1982. That progress has been achieved

---

[11] Task Force of the National Advisory Council on Alcohol Abuse and Alcoholism, *A Call to Action: Changing the Culture of Drinking at U.S. Colleges*, NIAAA, 2002, p. 24.

[12] *National Survey on Drug Use and Health* (2003), available at http://www.samhsa.gov/oas/p0000016.htm.

[13] Source of base data: U.S. Bureau of the Census.

[14] Available at http://monitoringthefuture.org.

[15] Source of base data: *Projections of Education Statistics to 2012*, Thirty-first Edition. U.S. Department of Education, National Center for Education Statistics, October 2002, http://nces.ed.gov/pubs2002/2002030.pdf.

[16] *The American Freshman Survey* (2003), sponsored by UCLA and the American Council on Education, available at http://www.gseis.ucla.edu/heri/freshman.htm.

even though the number of 16 to 20-year-olds licensed to drive has increased over 7% over the last decade to more than 12.4 million.[17]

While many factors explain this success, and there is still significant room for improvement, we believe that one of reasons for the progress of the last 20 years is that different groups have come together to create programs that work.

And those groups include members of our industry. I am happy to report that I could give each member of this committee the names of many people in your districts among our ranks that work with us on similar efforts. I hope you would agree that it is good work.

Last year, the Federal Trade Commission issued a report on alcohol beverage industry self-regulation in which it reviewed industry-sponsored alcohol awareness programs. The FTC commended these programs and pointed out that they are developed by professionals in the fields of education, medicine or alcohol abuse and that they follow approaches recommended by alcohol research.[18]

In discussing solutions and efforts that are yielding results, I would be remiss if I also didn't address a fundamental difference we have with some on the issue of advertising and teen drinking.

Advertising is not what causes youth to drink. In fact, since 1982, Anheuser–Busch's advertising expenditures have tripled, while teen drinking has declined 32 percent and teen drunk driving fatalities have declined 61 percent.

At the same time, our advertising is intended for adults, and those of us in the beer industry voluntarily undertake extensive steps to place our ads in adult programming. Our advertising is only placed in television, radio and magazines where the proportion of the audience above age 21 is reasonably expected to be 70% or higher. This standard reflects the demographics of the U.S. population, in which approximately 70% of the public is age 21 or older. The 2003 FTC report commended the industry's

[17] U.S. Department of Transportation, National Highway Traffic Safety Administration and Federal Highway Administration (2002).

[18] Federal Trade Commission, *Alcohol Marketing and Advertising–A Report to Congress*, September, 2003, p. 21.

self-regulation and also concluded that the industry did not target youth with its advertising.

As adults, we need to help youth navigate through an adult world, not try to pretend that adult activities don't exist. In the end, underage drinking is not an advertising issue, it's a family issue, and it's a societal issue.

As you know, the National Academy of Sciences also reviewed these issues in its 2003 report. We have some fundamental differences with some of the National Academy's recommendations.

Although the recent National Academy's recommendation to increase excise taxes is not part of our discussion here today, it is well known that the beer industry opposes such a measure; and I would like to take a brief moment to explain why.

Higher excise taxes are not an effective deterrent to abusive consumption or illegal underage drinking. The science on this issue was examined by the NIAAA in its 10th Special Report to Congress. Their conclusion is that no consensus exists in this debate. Research funded by the NIAAA indicates that teens are not impacted by higher taxes. Further, the research on the effects of higher taxes on college students is also cited in the NIAAA report, and it concludes, "The results suggested that alcohol prices were a less salient determinant of the drinking behavior of college students than they were in other populations." Finally, a study coauthored by one of the National Academy's panelists indicates that the effects of tax increases may be "considerably smaller than suggested in previous literature.[19] The bottom line is that we do not support this recommendation because there is no scientific consensus to show that it will reduce teen drinking. In addition, because excise taxes are highly regressive, a tax increase would force a large number of middle class adults who enjoy beer to bear an unfair and disproportional tax burden.

In closing, let me reiterate that the efforts I have focused on today include not only those supported by Anheuser–Busch and its beer

---

[19] Cook, P.J. and Moore, M.J., ''Environment and Persistence in Youthful Drinking Patterns,'' in *Risky Behavior Among Youths, An Economic Analysis*, edited by Jonathan Gruber, University of Chicago Press, National Bureau of Economic Research, 2001, pp. 375–437.

wholesalers, but also those supported by our colleagues at Miller, Coors, Heineken and other brewers.

We believe the best way to continue the progress made in the fight against underage drinking is through education, especially involving parents. And the collective investment we make in our youth will ensure their safe passage into adulthood.

* * *

[Attachments to Ms. Katz's statement follow:]

1. Statistical summary on progress in reducing alcohol abuse
2. Organizations/groups that endorse/support Anheuser–Busch alcohol awareness efforts
3. Anheuser–Busch national wholesaler accomplishments in implementing alcohol awareness programs
4. Beer Institute Advertising Code
5. Anheuser–Busch College Marketing Code
6. Driver's license guidebook provided to retailers [Retained in the Committee's official files.]
7. Examples of Anheuser–Busch alcohol awareness advertising

SIGNS OF PROGRESS

Underage Drinking

- 82 percent of adolescents (ages 12-17) do not drink.[20]
- The percentage of high-school seniors who reported having a drink in the last 30 days is at its lowest level since the study began in

[20] *2002 National Survey on Drug Use and Health*, an annual survey representative of the U.S. population age 12+ (2002 sample size included 68,126 individuals) conducted by the Substance Abuse and Mental Health Services Administration, U.S. Department of Health & Human Services, 2003. http://www.drugabusestatistics.samhsa. gov/ The National Survey on Drug Use and Health defines *current drinkers* as those who have had at least one drink in the past 30 days.

1975. The record-low in 2003 is 17 percent lower than in 1990, and down 32 percent since 1982.[21]

- The percentage of high-school seniors who reported having five or more drinks in a row in the last two weeks is 13 percent lower in 2003 than in 1990, and down 31 percent since 1982.
- The percentage of college freshmen who reported drinking beer frequently or occasionally is at its lowest level since record-keeping began in 1966. The record-low in 2003 is 21 percent lower than in 1990 and down 39 percent since 1982.[22]

Drunk Driving

- The number of fatalities in drunk-driving crashes has declined 24 percent since 1990 and 37 percent since 1982, going from 21,113 in 1982 to 13,406 in 2002.[23]
- The drunk-driving fatality rate per 100 million Vehicle Miles Traveled is down 64 percent since 1982.[24]
- The number of fatalities in teenage drunk-driving crashes has declined 36 percent since 1990 and 61 percent since 1982, going from 4,214 in 1982 to 1,651 in 2002.[22]

So What Does All This Mean?

- Nearly 20 million adolescents are doing the right thing by not drinking; 82 percent of 12-17 year-olds are not current drinkers.[19, 25]

---

[21] University of Michigan "Monitoring the Future" Study, sponsored by the National Institute on Drug Abuse, U S Department of Health & Human Services, 2003. http://www.monitoringthefuture.org/.

[22] *American Freshman Survey*, sponsored by UCLA and the American Council on Education, 2004; http://www.gseis.ucla.edu/heri/heri. html.

[23] National Highway Traffic Safety Administration, U.S. Department of Transportation, 2003.

[24] Sources: National Highway Traffic Safety Administration, U.S. Department of Transportation, 2003; http://www-nrd.nhtsa.dot.gov/ pdf/nrd-30/NCSA/Rpts/2003/Assess02.pdf.

[25] Source of base data: U.S. Bureau of the Census.

- In 2003, there were nearly 410,000 fewer high-school seniors who reported past-month drinking than did in 1982.[20, 26]
- There were 4,200 fewer drunk-driving fatalities in 2002 than there were in 1990, and there were 7,700 fewer drunk-driving fatalities in 2002 than in 1982.[22]
- There were 900 fewer teen drunk-driving fatalities in 2002 than there were in 1990, and 2,500 fewer teen drunk-driving fatalities in 2002 than in 1982.[22]

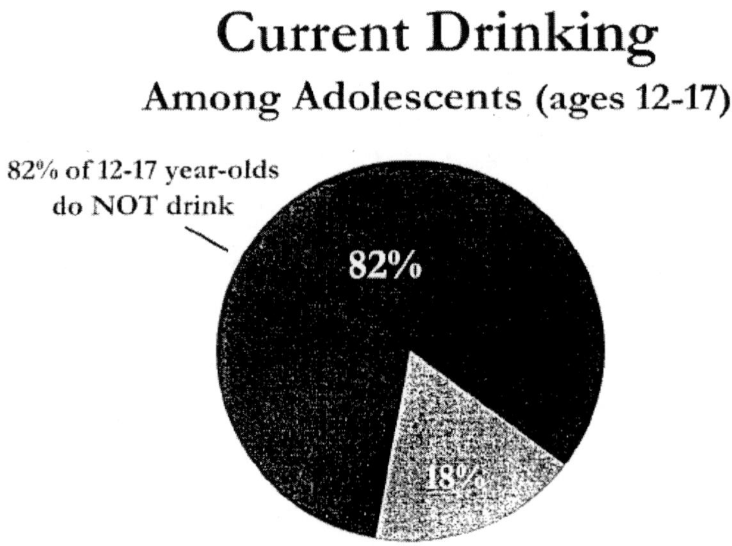

Source: *2002 National Survey on Drug Use and Health*, an annual survey representative of the U.S. population age 12+ (2002 sample size included 68,126 individuals) conducted by the Substance Abuse and Mental Health Services Administration, U.S. Department of Health & Human Services, 2003. http:// www.drugabusestatistics.samhsa.gm /

The National Survey on Drug Use and Health defines current drinkers as those who have had at least one drink in the past 30 days. Revised 2/6/04.

---

[26] Source of base data: *Projections of Education Statistics to 2012*, Thirty-first Edition. U.S. Department of Education, National Center for Education Statistics, October 2002. http://nces.ed.gov/pubs2002/2002030.pdf/

Drinking Among High School Seniors

Percent Who Have Consumed Alcohol in the Last Month

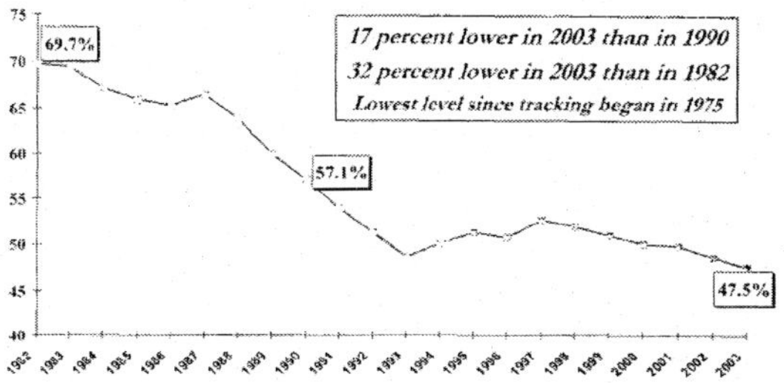

Source: The University of Michigan, *Monitoring the Future Study*, sponsored by the National Institute on Drug Abuse, U.S. Department of Health and Human Services.

Surveys of nationally representative samples of American high school seniors were begun in 1975, making the class of 2003 the 29th such class surveyed. Surveys of eighth- and 10th-graders were added to the design in 1991, making the 2003 nationally representative samples the 13th such classes surveyed. The sample sizes in 2003 are 17,000 eighth-graders located in 141 schools, 16,200 10th-graders located in 129 schools, and 15,200 12th-graders located in 122 schools, for a total of 48,500 students in 392 schools overall. The samples are drawn to be representative of students in private and public secondary schools across the United States, selected with probability proportionate to estimated class size, to yield separate, nationally representative samples of students from each of the three grade levels. http://www.monitoringthefuture.org/ Accessed 12/19/03.

Drinking Among High School Seniors

Percent Who Reported Drinking 5 or More Drinks In A Row in the Last 2 Weeks

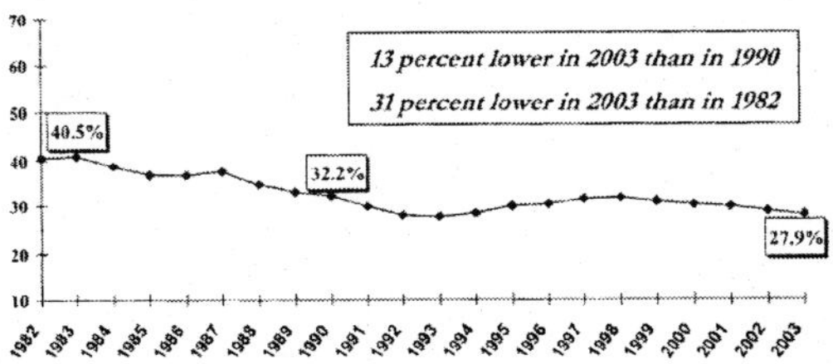

Source: The University of Michigan, *Monitoring the Future Study*, sponsored by the National Institute on Drug Abuse, U.S. Department of Health and Human Services.

Surveys of nationally representative samples of American high school seniors were begun in 1975, making the class of 2003 the 29th such class surveyed. Surveys of eighth- and 10th-graders were added to the design in 1991, making the 2003 nationally representative samples the 13th such classes surveyed. The sample sizes in 2003 are 17,000 eighth-graders located in 141 schools, 16,200 10th-graders located in 129 schools, and 15,200 12th-graders located in 122 schools, for a total of 48,500 students in 392 schools overall. The samples are drawn to be representative of students in private and public secondary schools across the United States, selected with probability proportionate to estimated class size, to yield separate, nationally representative samples of students from each of the three grade levels. http://www.monitoringthefuture.org/ Accessed 12/19/03.

Percentage of College Freshmen Who Drink Beer Frequently or Occasionally

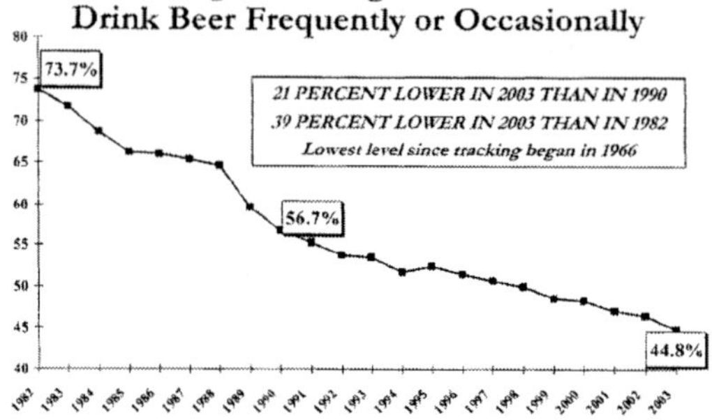

Source: *The American Freshman Survey*, sponsored by UCLA and the American Council on Education and conducted by the Higher Education Research Institute at UCLA's Graduate School of Education & Information Studies, is the nation's largest and longest empirical study of higher education, with a sample of more than 1,800 institutions and more than 11 million students since its inception in 1966. Now in its 38th year, the UCLA Survey is the nation's longest- running and most comprehensive assessment of student attitudes and plans. The fall 2003 survey sample included responses from 276,449 students at 413 of the nation's baccalaureate colleges and universities, and is representative of the 1.2 million first-time, full -time students entering all four-year colleges and universities as freshmen in 2003. "Frequently or occasionally" is self-reported as drinking beer one or more rimes in the past year, http / /www gseis.ucla.edu/heri/heri.html. Revised 1/26/04.

Total Fatalities in Drunk-Driving Crashes

Driver BAC of .08 and higher

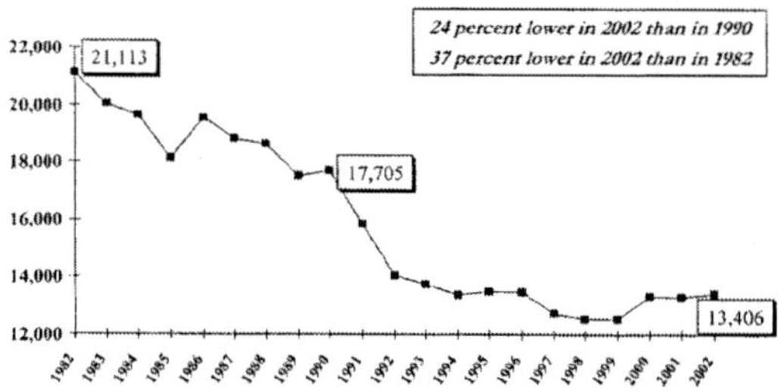

Source: National Highway Traffic Safety Administration, U.S. Department of Transportation. 2003 Drunk-driving fatalities represent the total number of people (occupants and non-occupants) killed in motor vehicle traffic crashes in which at least one driver had a BAC of .08 or higher.

Note: These data reflect NHTSA's new methodology in estimating missing BAC test result data. The old method computed die chance of involvement along definite categories (0, 0.01 to 0.09, and (1.10+) of BAC while the new method, multiple imputation, imputes actual values of BAC (0 to 0.94). NHTSA's new methodology improves the scope of alcohol involvement statistics generated by the Fatality Analysis Reporting System (FARS). Revised 1/26/04.

Total Drunk-Driving Fatalities
Per 100 Million Vehicle Miles Traveled

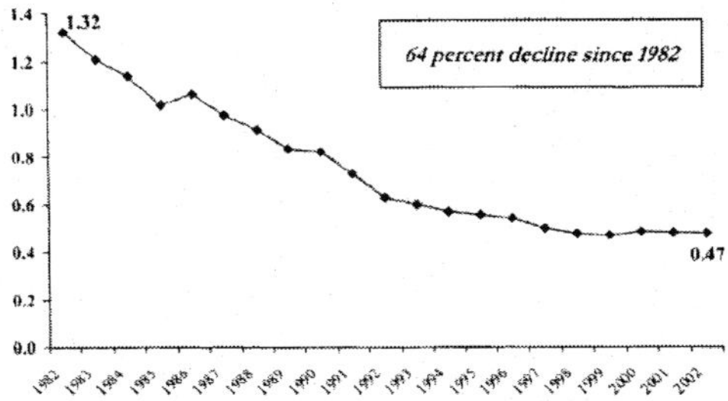

Source: National Highway Traffic Safety Administration. U S. Department of Transportation, 2003; http://www-nrd.nhtsa.dot.gov/pdf/nrd.30/NCSA/TSFAnn/TSF2003.pdf.; http://www-nrd. nhtsa.dot.gov/pdf/nrd-30/NCSA/Rpts/2003/Assess02.pdf. Drunk-driving fatalities rep-resent the total number of people (occupants and non-occupants) killed in motor vehicle traffic crashes in which at least one driver had a BAC of .08 or higher.

Note: Drunk-driving data reflect NHTSA's new methodology in estimating missing BAC test result data. The old method computed the chance of involvement along definite categories (0, 0.01 to 0.09. and 0.10+) of BAC while the new method, multiple imputation, imputes actual values of BAC (0 to 0.94). NHTSA's new methodology improves the scope of alcohol involvement statistics generated by the Fatality Analysis Reporting System (FARS). Revised 1/26/04.

Total Fatalities in Teen Drunk-Driving Crashes
Driver BAC of .08 and higher

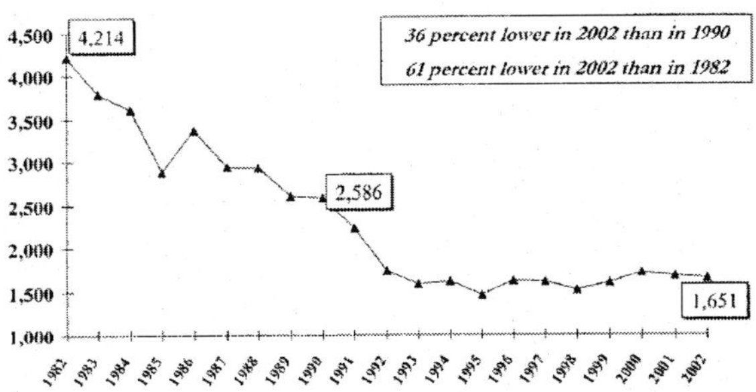

Source: National Highway Traffic Safety Administration. U S. Department of Transportation, 2003. Drunk-driving fatalities represent the total number of people (occupants and non-occupants) killed in motor vehicle traffic crashes in which at least one driver had a BAC of .08 or higher.

Note: These data reflect NHTSA's new methodology in estimating missing BAC test result data. The old method computed the chance of involvement along definite categories (0, 0.01 to 0.09. and 0.10+) of BAC while the new method, multiple imputation, imputes actual values of BAC (0 to 0.94). NHTSA's new methodology improves the scope of alcohol involvement statistics generated by the Fatality Analysis Reporting System (FARS).

Partners

Here is a list of organizations with whom we have partnered on alcohol awareness programs and projects, or who have distributed our program materials.

- American Association of State Colleges and Universities
- American Council on Alcoholism
- American School Counselor Association
- BACCHUS & GAMMA Peer Education Network
- Big Brothers Big Sisters of Mississippi
- Florida Governor's Mentoring Initiative
- Florida Highway Patrol
- Florida Literacy Coalition
- Florida Student Association
- Illinois State Police
- Inter-Association Task Force on Alcohol and other Substance Abuse Issues
- International Association of Chiefs of Police
- Korean American Coalition
- Korean Health Education, Information and Research Center
- Mississippi Boys and Girls Club
- Mississippi Mentoring Network
- National Association of State Universities and Land-Grant Colleges
- National Clearinghouse for Alcohol and Drug Information
- National Collegiate Athletic Association
- National Commission Against Drunk Driving
- National Council of Negro Women
- National Highway Traffic Safety Administration (NHTSA)
- National Rural Alcohol and Drug Abuse Network
- National Safe Boating Council

- National School Boards Association
- National Social Norms Resource Center
- Optimist International
- Organization of Chinese Americans, Inc.
- Provident Counseling
- State Attorneys General: Indiana, Nevada, New Mexico, Texas
- State Law Enforcement Chiefs Association (FL)
- Take Stock in Children
- The Betty Ford Center
- The Caron Foundation
- U.S. Hispanic Chamber of Commerce
- U.S. Junior Chamber of Commerce (Jaycees)
- Alcohol Medical Scholars Program

NATIONWIDE WHOLESALER EFFORTS 2002

Every year, Anheuser-Busch wholesalers work with local businesses and organizations to initiate alcohol awareness activities in communities nationwide. When it comes to preventing alcohol abuse, including drunk driving and underage drinking, We All Make A Difference. In 2002 alone, our wholesalers accomplished the following:

Underage Drinking Prevention: Stopping Sales to Minors

- ✓ Distributed more than 350,000 Family Talk About Drinking program materials -- to help parents prevent underage drinking. Nearly 3.9 million Family Talk materials have been distributed since 1990.
- ✓ Provided more than 7.1 million wristbands, 170,000 We ID Cards and 156,000 LD. books {with color photographs of driver's licenses from all 50 states and Canada) to help servers and sellers

of alcohol beverages effectively identify those patrons of legal purchase age and stop sales to minors. More than 22 million wristbands, 858,000 We ID Cards and 1.1 million I.D. books have been distributed since 1990.

- ✓ Hosted more than 950 in-school presentations by speakers who educate and motivate young people to make smart choices and respect themselves and the law. More than 321,000 students attended these presentations in 2002. Wholesalers have hosted more than 4,700 in-school presentations since 1998, and more than 1.4 million students attended these presentations.
- ✓ Placed nearly 13,000 advertisements in local newspapers, in-stadium signage, on billboards, Internet, radio and television, to help prevent underage drinking.

Drunk Driving Prevention: Saving Lives

- ✓ More than 530 Anheuser-Busch wholesalers conducted designated driver programs in 2002.
- ✓ More than 200 wholesalers participated in the 2002 Budweiser Designated Driver Holiday Sweepstakes to encourage the use of designated drivers during the holidays.
- ✓ Placed more than 20,000 advertisements encouraging the use of designated drivers.
- ✓ Instructed, through server training programs, nearly 25,000 bartenders, waiters, waitresses, convenience store clerks and home party hosts on responsible-serving techniques to help them prevent alcohol abuse, drunk driving and underage drinking. More than 300,000 servers have been trained by Anheuser-Busch wholesalers since 1989.
- ✓ Provided more than 52,000 free cab rides home from bars and restaurants. More than 420,000 rides have been provided since 1989.

Responsible Drinking: Preventing Alcohol Abuse

- ✓ Placed more than 44,000 advertisements in local newspapers, in-stadium signage, on billboards, Internet, radio and television, reminding adult consumers to drink responsibly. Wholesalers have run nearly 443,000 responsibility ads since 1989.
- ✓ Implemented more than 1,000 Good Sport programs to promote positive behavior among more than 34.6 million attendees of sporting events, fairs and community festivals.

College Programs: Promoting Positive Social Norms

- ✓ Participated in alcohol awareness and education programs with 473 colleges and universities. More than 686,000 students participated in these programs.
- ✓ Participated in National Collegiate Alcohol Awareness Week programs on 161 campuses.
- ✓ Implemented the College Talk program on 233 campuses.
- ✓ Provided We ID materials to servers and sellers in 151 college and university markets, to help them effectively identify patrons of the legal purchase age and stop sales to minors.
- ✓ Implemented college and university designated driver programs on 140 campuses.
- ✓ The "True or False, '/"Magic Ball Social Norms Campaign was implemented on 152 campuses.
- ✓ Placed more than 2,400 alcohol awareness and education social norms advertisements on college and university campuses.[27]

---

[27] This information is based on the results of a survey of all Anheuser-Busch wholesalers, conducted by Product Acceptance & Research, 2003.

BEER INSTITUTE: ADVERTISING AND MARKETING CODE

Introduction

Beer is a legal beverage meant to be consumed responsibly. Its origins are ancient, and it has held a respected position in nearly every culture and society since the dawn of recorded history.

Advertising is a legitimate effort by brewers to make consumers aware of the particular types, brands, and prices of malt beverages that are available.

Beer distribution in the United States is subject to extensive laws and regulations, enforced by federal, state, and local governments. Federal and state law establishes a three-tiered distribution system for beer, composed of brewers, wholesale distributors, and retail sellers. Companies in each tier of this distribution system are required by law to maintain their commercial independence. The Beer Institute encourages all with whom brewers do business to adhere to the law, as well as this voluntary Advertising and Marketing Code, which is provided annually to the independent distributors which sell their products.

Three basic principles, which have long been reflected in the policies of the brewing industry, continue to underlie these Guidelines. First, Beer advertising should not suggest directly or indirectly that any of the laws applicable to the sale and consumption of beer should not be complied with. Second, brewers should adhere to standards of candor and good taste applicable to all commercial advertising. Third, brewers are responsible corporate citizens, sensitive to the problems of the society in which they exist, and their advertising should reflect that fact.

Brewers strongly oppose abuse or inappropriate consumption of their products.

Guidelines

1. These guidelines apply to all brewer advertising and marketing materials, including Internet and other cyberspace media. These guidelines do not apply to educational materials or televised, printed, or audio messages of a non-brand specific nature; nor to materials or messages designed specifically to address issues of alcohol abuse or underage drinking.
2. Beer advertising and marketing materials should portray beer in a responsible manner.
   - a Beer advertising and marketing materials should not portray, encourage, or condone drunk driving.
   - b Beer advertising and marketing materials should not depict situations where beer is being consumed excessively, in an irresponsible way, or in any way illegally.
   - c Beer advertising and marketing materials should not portray persons in a state of intoxication or in any way suggest that intoxication is acceptable conduct.
   - d Beer advertising and marketing materials should not portray or imply illegal activity of any kind.
   - e Retail outlets or other places portrayed in advertising should be depicted as well kept and respectable establishments.
3. Brewers are committed to a policy and practice of responsible advertising and marketing. As a part of this philosophy, beer advertising and marketing materials are intended for adults of legal purchase age who choose to drink.
   - a. Beer advertising and marketing materials should not employ any symbol, language, music, gesture, or cartoon character that is intended to appeal primarily to persons below the legal purchase age. Advertising or marketing material has a "primary appeal" to persons under the legal purchase age if it has special attractiveness to such persons beyond the general attractiveness it has for persons above the legal purchase age.

b. Beer advertising and marketing materials should not employ any entertainment figure or group that is intended to appeal primarily to persons below the legal purchase age.
c. Beer advertising and marketing materials should not depict Santa Claus.
d. Beer advertising and marketing materials shall only be placed in magazines, on television, or on radio where at least 70% of the audience is expected to be adults of legal purchase age. The brewer placing advertising or marketing materials in magazines, on television, or on radio shall conduct periodic after-the-fact audits, at least semi-annually, of a random portion of its placements. If a brewer learns that a placement did not meet the Code Standard it will take steps to prevent a reoccurrence. A placement will be considered reasonable if the audience composition data reviewed prior to placement met the percentages set forth above. What constitutes a reasonable basis for placement depends on the medium and available data for that medium. Buying guidelines for the implementation of this section will be distributed in conformance with the dissemination provisions of this code.
e. To help insure that the people shown in beer advertising are and appear to be above the legal purchase age, models and actors employed should be a minimum of 25 years old, substantiated by proper identification, and should reasonably appear to be over 21 years of age.
f. Beer should not be advertised or marketed at any event where most of the audience is reasonably expected to be below the legal purchase age. This guideline does not prevent brewers from erecting advertising and marketing materials at or near facilities that are used primarily for adult-oriented events, but which occasionally may be used for an event where most attendees are under age 21.
g. No beer identification, including logos, trademarks, or names should be used or licensed for use on clothing, toys, games or

game equipment, or other materials intended for use primarily by persons below the legal purchase age.

h. Brewers recognize that parents play a significant role in educating their children about the legal and responsible use of alcohol and may wish to prevent their children from accessing Internet Web sites without parental supervision. To facilitate this exercise of parental responsibility, Beer Institute will provide to manufacturers of parent control software the names and Web site addresses of all member-company Web sites. Additionally, brewers will require disclosure of a viewer's date of birth at the entry to their websites and will post reminders at appropriate locations in their Web site indicating that brewer products are intended only for those of legal purchase age. These locations include entrance into the Web site, purchase points within the Web site, and access into adult-oriented locations within the Web site, such as virtual bars.

4. Beer consumption is intended as a complement to leisure or social activity. Beer advertising and marketing activities should not associate or portray beer drinking before or during activities which require a high degree of alertness or coordination.
5. Beer advertising and marketing materials should not make exaggerated product representations.
   a. Beer advertising and marketing materials should not convey the impression that a beer has special or unique qualities if in fact it does not.
   b. Beer advertising and marketing materials should make no scientifically unsubstantiated health claims.
   c. Beer may be portrayed to be part of personal and social experiences and activities. Nevertheless, beer advertising and marketing materials should contain no claims or representations that individuals cannot obtain social, professional, educational, athletic, or financial success or status without beer consumption; nor should they claim or represent that

individuals cannot solve social, personal, or physical problems without beer consumption.

6. Beer advertising and marketing materials should reflect generally accepted contemporary standards of good taste.
   a. Beer advertising and marketing materials should not contain any lewd or indecent language or images.
   b. Beer advertising and marketing materials should not portray sexual passion, promiscuity, or any other amorous activity as a result of consuming beer.
   c. Beer advertising and marketing materials should not employ religion or religious themes.
7. Beer advertising and marketing materials should not disparage competing beers. In the event comparisons are drawn between competing beers, the claims made should be truthful and of value to consumers.
8. Beer advertising and marketing materials should never suggest that competing beers contain objectionable additives or ingredients.
9. Beer advertising and marketing materials should not refer to any intoxicating effect that the product may produce.
10. Beer advertising and marketing materials should not depict the act of drinking.
11. Beer advertising and marketing materials should not show littering or otherwise improper disposal of beer containers, unless the scenes are used clearly to promote anti-littering and/or recycling campaigns.
12. College marketing: Beer advertising and marketing activities on college and university campuses, or in college media, should not portray consumption of beer as being important to education, nor shall advertising directly or indirectly degrade studying. Beer may be advertised and marketed on college campuses or at college-sponsored events only when permitted by appropriate college policy.
    a. On-campus promotions/sponsorships

1. Company sponsored events: Company sponsorship of on-campus events or company promotions at on-campus licensed retail establishments shall be limited to events conducted in accord with this Code, state law, and applicable institutional policies. In their content and implementation, company on-campus promotions and sponsorships shall not encourage the irresponsible, excessive, underage, or otherwise illegal consumption of alcohol.
2. Branded products: Beer-branded promotional products such as key chains, clothing, posters, or other tangible goods designed to promote specific beer brands, are intended only for adults of legal purchase age. Distribution of these items will therefore take place only at licensed retail establishments or where distribution is limited to those over the legal purchase age, and otherwise conforms to applicable laws and institutional policies.
3. Tastings: Tasting events at which product samples are provided should occur at licensed retail establishments or where distribution is limited to those over the legal purchase age, and otherwise conforms to applicable laws and institutional policies.

b. Company sales representatives: Company sales representatives who undertake sales calls on or near a college campus must be at least of legal purchase age, and shall conduct sales activities in conformity with this Code.

13. Billboards: Billboard advertisements by brewers shall be located at least 500 linear feet from established and conspicuously identified elementary or secondary schools, places of worship, or public playgrounds.
14. Product placement: Movies and television programs frequently portray consumption of alcohol and related signage and props in their productions. Brewers encourage producers to seek company approval before using their products, signage, or other props in

artistic productions. While producers sometimes seek prior approval from the companies, the final artistic and editorial decisions concerning product portrayal are always within the exclusive control of the movie or television producers.

With regard to those who seek company approval, product placement will be guided by the following principles:

a. Case. by Case Approval: Where their approval is sought, brewers will approve or reject product placement in specific projects or scenes on a case by case basis, based upon the information provided by the movie or television program's producers.
b. Portrayal of drinking and driving: Brewers discourage the illegal or irresponsible consumption of their products in connection with driving. Consistent with that philosophy, the companies will not approve product placement where the characters engage in illegal or irresponsible consumption of their products in connection with driving.
c. Underage drinking: Brewers discourage underage drinking and do not intend for their products to be purchased or consumed illegally by minors. Consistent with that philosophy, the companies will not approve product placement which portrays purchase or consumption of their products by persons who are under the legal purchase age.
d. Primary appeal to minors; Brewers discourage underage drinking and do not intend for their products to be purchased or consumed illegally by minors. Consistent with that philosophy, the companies will not approve product placement where the primary character(s) are under the legal purchase age or the primary theme(s) arc, because of their content or presentation, particularly attractive to children.
e. Portraying alcoholism/alcohol abuse: Brewers do not want their products to be abused. Consistent with that philosophy, the companies will not approve product placement where characters use their products irresponsibly or abusively or

where alcoholism is portrayed, unless the depiction supports a responsible-use message.

Code Compliance and Dissemination

Bach member of the Beer Institute is committed to the philosophy of the Code and is committed to compliance with the Code. When the Beer Institute receives complaints with regard to any member's advertising or marketing, it has long been its practice and it will continue to be its practice to promptly refer such complaints in writing to the member company for its review and action. To facilitate this end, the Beer Institute maintains an 800 number (1-800-379-2739). A copy of this code shall continue to be given to every brewery employee, wholesale distributor and outside agency whose responsibilities include advertising and marketing beer, as well as to any outside party who might request it.

Beer Institute
122 C Street, N.W., Suite 750
Washington, DC 20001-2150
202-737-2337

College Marketing Code

Anheuser–Busch is committed to the responsible enjoyment of its alcohol beverage products by adults of legal purchase and drinking age. This commitment is particularly important in the environment of the American college campus, where many young adults are making decisions about beer that might remain with them for the rest of their lives.

We believe college students 21 and over have the right to enjoy beer responsibly as do other adults in our society. In fact, the vast majority of America's 89 million adult beer drinkers enjoy beer in a responsible manner that is consistent with a healthy lifestyle. We also believe that college students under 21 should respect the state laws that prohibit them from purchasing and consuming alcohol beverages.

Anheuser–Busch historically has supported programs to discourage underage drinking and to remind those of legal drinking age to drink responsibly . . . programs such as BACCHUS (Boost Alcohol Consciousness Concerning the Health of University Students), the NCAA Foundation's "Choices" grant program, and National Collegiate Alcohol Awareness Week.

It has long been our belief and practice that our marketing and advertising programs reflect our commitment to responsible enjoyment of beer by adults of legal age. While numerous studies have demonstrated that alcohol beverage advertising does not cause alcohol abuse or underage drinking, we have developed the following college marketing guidelines to formalize our commitment to encourage responsible use of our products and to discourage underage drinking.

The guidelines do not apply to educational materials, televised, printed or audio messages which do not have as their principal message promotion of a beer brand, nor materials or messages designed to address issues of alcohol abuse or underage drinking.

In all cases, Anheuser–Busch marketing efforts which occur on campus will be conducted in accordance with any college or university regulations which apply to the sale and marketing of alcohol beverage products.

Advertising

Advertising is defined as a message placed in traditional media such as television, radio, magazines, newspapers, and signs. "Campus media" includes any publication that is intended for distribution primarily to undergraduate college students. Campus media does not include any radio, television or cable television stations that also reach a general audience in the community.

When purchasing advertising in campus media, Anheuser–Busch will do so within the following guidelines:

- All beer advertising will adhere to the guidelines contained in the Brewing Industry Advertising Code.
- All beer advertising placed in campus media will comply with any guidelines set forth by the University or College Administration.

Event Sponsorship and Promotion

Event sponsorship and promotion is defined as providing financial or other resources in exchange for display of and recognition for specific brand names in conjunction with the event.

Events on Campus

Anheuser–Busch will limit its event sponsorship and promotion on campus to licensed retail establishments and those activities open to the general public, such as intercollegiate athletics, entertainment events and charity fund-raisers where most of the audience is reasonably expected to be above the legal purchase age. For all such events, management of the event must agree to implement and enforce an effective system of checking identification and adhering to minimum purchase age laws in place, if beer is sold or served.

Spring Break

At Spring Break destination locations, Anheuser–Busch will not conduct beer advertising, event sponsorships or promotions on beaches or at other outdoor locations or non-licensed premises where most of the audience is reasonably expected to be below the legal purchase age.

Product Sampling

Sampling of Anheuser–Busch products on campus among consumers of legal drinking age where allowed by law, will be limited to circumstances meeting the following criteria.

- The event must be limited to the premises of licensed retail accounts and the management of the event must agree that the event will be conducted in accordance with school policy.
- The management of the event must agree to establish and enforce reasonable limits as to time and quantity of consumption.

Promotional Materials

Beer-branded promotional materials are defined as posters, calendars, articles of clothing, glassware and novelty items such as towels, pens, key chains, buttons and the like designed to promote the sale of specific beer brands. Anheuser–Busch beer-branded materials are intended only for adults of legal purchase age. Anheuser–Busch will limit its free distribution of promotional materials on campus to circumstances meeting the following criteria:

- Distribution must be at a licensed retail establishment or during activities at a venue open to the general public where most of the audience is reasonably expected to be above the legal purchase age.
- Persons in charge of distribution must agree to make a good faith effort to limit distribution to those of legal purchase age.

Company Sales Representatives

Anheuser–Busch sales personnel must be above the minimum purchase age and limit their calls on campus to licensed retail establishments.

Dissemination of Guidelines

A significant percentage of marketing activities at or near college campuses are undertaken, not by Anheuser–Busch, but by wholesalers who distribute our products. They are independent businessmen and women who have a strong commitment to the communities and the colleges they serve. And, like Anheuser–Busch, they also are committed to responsible marketing practices. We encourage them to follow these guidelines.

These guidelines are to be distributed annually by Anheuser–Busch to the following:

- University and college administrators;
- Wholesalers who distribute Anheuser–Busch beers;
- All Anheuser–Busch sales and marketing personnel.

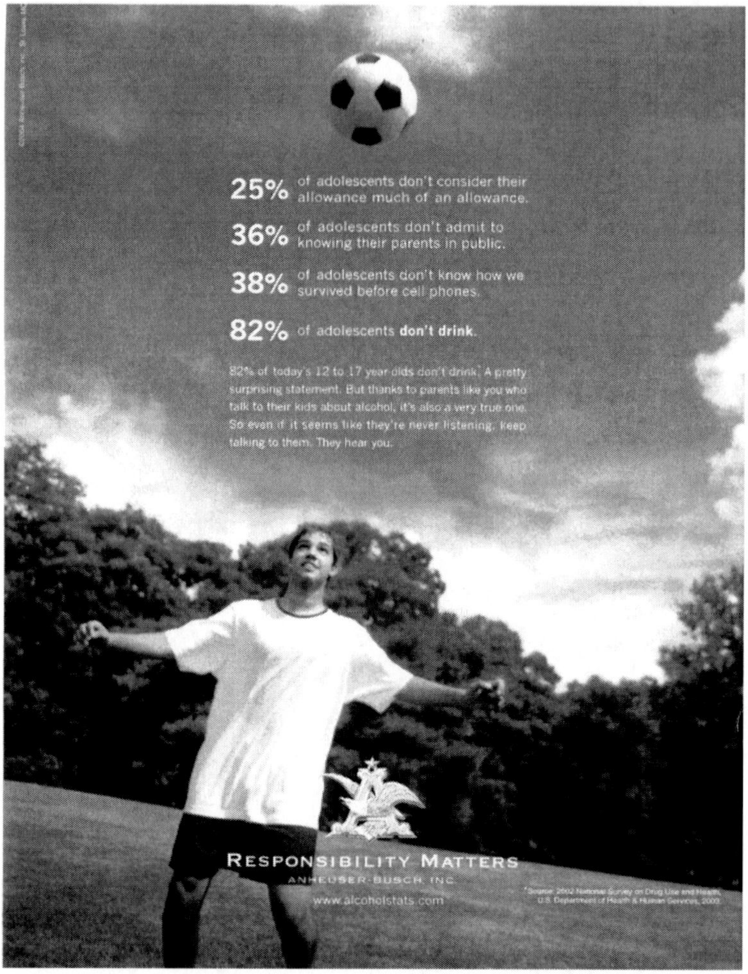

Mr. Osborne. Thank you very much. We'll now begin questioning. And in deference to Ms. Woolsey's schedule—she has another hearing—I would like to call on her at this time.

Ms. Woolsey. Thank you very much, coach, for letting me do this.

We call him "coach," too, Mr. Newton.

[Laughter.]

Ms. Woolsey. I have a question. Mr. Newton, if SADD had been in existence when you were in school, would it have made any difference to you? Would you have joined? Would you have supported?

How would it have mattered?

Mr. Newton. I think it would have been an opportunity to intervene on me early. At that time there were no programs in schools and it was a heavy drinking environment in my high school. So it could have been an opportunity for early intervention. So I think it really has some value.

To carry that—the biggest concern I have with young people is the mixed message. They see so many messages to drink by the time they're 18, and the drinking age is 21 in America, so it's a contradiction that they have a hard time working through. But it would have been an opportunity for early intervention for me.

Ms. Woolsey. OK. Thank you very much.

Jacqueline, tell us from your perspective and SADD's perspective, what part do parents play? How important are parents in—

Ms. Hackett. Certainly, the parents are very influential to their children, and that's why we need to inform the parents of the dangers of underage drinking. We need to let the parents know the statistics about how many youth are dying and how it affects all of their lives, and we need the parents to send the message that students should not be drinking.

Ms. Woolsey. So how are we going to get that message to the parents and to youth? Have you—what kind of—would a national media campaign work? Does it work with the drug programs? I mean, would it work?

Ms. Hackett. Absolutely.

Ms. Woolsey. And what would it act like?

Ms. Hackett. There is a lot of media centered toward youth, and youth are very influenced by newspapers, by the TV, and by magazines. And we need to act against that and send youth a positive message and help them make the right decisions about underage drinking.

Ms. Woolsey. Well, could you comment on the ad we just saw?

Because I can't believe that somebody that was old enough to drink in the first place is sneaking out of the house and putting makeup on. I mean, if they're a 21-year-old. So how does that—is that a message that worked?

Ms. Hackett. We need to use a kind of messaging—when people are in the media that are drinking, they're good- looking, they're smart, they're athletic. We need to do something to counteract that.

We have to make hip ads. An example would be the truth. It's those kind of ads that are reaching the youth and helping them to make their own decisions. So I think that's a campaign that we could definitely look toward making modifications to that work on the underage drinking aspects.

Ms. Woolsey. OK. Thank you very much. I think I'm going to yield back, because I really have to go someplace else, but I want to thank you all so very much. You've been very, very helpful to us. Thank you.

Mr. Osborne. Thank you, Ms. Woolsey. I'll just ask a few questions now. One statistic I ran across a few years ago—I think it's fairly accurate—is that by the time a young person is 21 years of age, they've watched roughly 2 years, not of television, but 2 years of commercials. That's a pretty powerful influence, 2 years out of 21, or even if it's a year or year-and-a-half. And I'd like to have you think with me a little bit as to what percentage of those commercials have to do with alcohol. Probably out of 2 years, a few months, you know, right? That would be fair. And out of those few months, how many de-glamorized alcohol and how many of them have glamorized? How many of them have involved young people who are, as was mentioned by Ms. Hackett, athletic, attractive, having a good time?

I certainly applaud you, Ms. Katz, for the commercial that you showed us. I think that was good. There was one other commercial on the Super Bowl that showed a rewind of what happens when you use drugs and alcohol that was one of the most watched. I think it was the most impressive to young people. But on the other hand, we had the dog biting the guy. We had the horse, flatulent horse, which appeals to probably somewhat of a juvenile sense of humor, and over and over and over again.

So there is a cumulative effect here. And it definitely impresses people. And I don't question your intentions. I don't question the industry's intentions. But the long-term effect has been a wearing down of sensibility to the destructiveness of alcohol.

Bob, I'd just like to ask you, you said mixed messages. Would you flesh that out a little bit? I know you may have some thoughts on exactly what might be done that would make that a little bit more effective.

Mr. Newton. Well, I agree with you. I think there is an association that young people see as alcohol being very glamorous. This is what successful people—this is how they celebrate. And I think they develop attitudes from seeing those messages.

I think to combat that—and as I said earlier, those young girls, those eighth grade girls, I really believe they didn't know alcohol was a depressant and a powerful drug. And I sincerely agree with that the earlier a person drinks alcohol, the physiological and the psychological impairment is devastating. A lot of them won't even get through school. There will be major, major negative consequences.

I think we need, as I mentioned earlier, we need a media campaign to combat all the positive messages that are sent with the association of alcohol, and I think that's one solution.

Mr. Osborne. OK. Thank you. I don't know how to say The Honorable Molinari, but anyway, I recognize your former status. Do you have any objective analysis of some of the data that you have presented? In other words, the effects of the counteractive measures where some outside agency has actually come in and audited and tried to determine how effective what you're doing has been?

Ms. Molinari. Sure. Absolutely, Mr. Chairman. As I said, all our current programs right now have an independent evaluation as part of it. And I daresay for a lot of alcohol prevention programs, they do not. We do. Some of our evaluators include for the Alcohol 101 Plus that's currently in the field right now, part of our evaluation committee consists of NIAAA and the Department of Education.

They will come back together in a very short period of time and consistently monitor progress. We're embarking on a several hundred thousand dollar program with the University of New York where we're going to sit down, and the chancellor has already agreed, where we're going to use these programs at different points of a college career and come back and on different college campuses perform evaluations with outside auditors and outside agencies.

A lot of our programs have been audited by the Pacific Institute and evaluated by the Pacific Institute. The University of Florida and George

Mason University. And yes, some of them, sir, have not been audited by professionals. But I challenge anyone sitting here today to look at this, the Brandon Story. This is the program that I got involved in as a Member of Congress. Brandon has toured all over the United States and spoken to high school students, particularly around prom and at graduation time. He barely can speak. He can barely walk anymore. He tells the story dramatically of the irresponsible decision he made, blames no one for hitting a tree and lost all his life dreams. And you know what, Mr. Chairman, I have been a part of that real evolution. When high school students come down and say, it's one instance, but it's duplicated, that just sticks in my mind. A group of girls before—because girls are the fastest rising binge drinkers in the United States today and of great concern—a jar full of change and said, wanted to let you know, we were giving this to John to go out and buy alcohol after the prom, and after we heard what happened to you, we're taking this money back and we're going to go get our nails done for the prom.

So most of our programs are very well expert analyzed. And some of them where I have sat in SPEAK-UP organizations on college campuses where we've worked with the athletes as role models, I have seen them save lives, sir.

Mr. Osborne. OK. Thank you. My time is up. Mr. Keller.

Mr. Keller. Thank you, Mr. Vice Chairman. And I want to begin by thanking you for your leadership, for bringing this issue before our Committee and being largely responsible for having this hearing today.

There's probably nobody I respect more in Congress than Coach Osborne. I refer to him as our E.F. Hutton Congressman. When he talks, everybody stops and listens. But I have to say that I don't quite share Coach Osborne's skepticism about what the industry is doing. And he mentioned Anheuser-Busch, for example, in his opening remarks.

And let me just tell you why. In my district of Orlando, Florida, the local Budweiser distributor is called Wayne Dench, and the president is a young man named John Williams, and they spend $42,000 a year there to help combat underage drinking, and it makes a big difference. And I'll just give you just three little examples that I'm personally familiar with.

We have a program in Central Florida called "Tow to Go." And if you're out at a bar and you're underage or even legal age, and you can't drive, you just call AAA and they send out a truck and they take you and your car home, no questions asked. And the beer distributor picks it up. And it saved 1,400 lives last year. Fourteen hundred drunks used it. And they pick up the tab. If you don't want your car towed, they have a similar service with a cab.

They send speakers to the different high schools as well. Congresswoman Molinari mentioned Brandon. And I was there and met Brandon, and I went to Winter Park High School with him.

And I tell you, I got up in front of those kids and gave my best I Have a Dream speech, and, you know, I'm not far removed from you, and I'm only 30 years old. And someone who was a jury trial lawyer before I got this job and now a politician. I have a sense of when I'm connecting with a crowd. And let me tell you, I did not connect with that crowd. It was like, whatever.

And when this young man got up and told his story, wow, they were blown away. And you could hear a pin drop. And that's because the local beer distributors cared about it and help fund it with Congresswoman Molinari's organization. $42,000 a year. Don't have to do it. Not doing it because there's a law. Not doing it because there's some statute. They're doing it because it's the right thing to do.

So I'm optimistic that working together, we can build partnerships to win this battle and take it on head on.

Let me ask Mr. Newton, let me ask you a question. I'm going to ask the same of Mrs. Katz here, and that is, on the issue of educating young people, I'm real interested in the age group where it's most successful. I know that you have spoke to kids at all levels, and my gut reaction as a layman sitting up here looking at this issue is that you probably have more success focusing your resources and time with middle schoolers or ninth and tenth grade than you would at a fraternity party with 20-year-olds. But you tell me. You've been in the field. Where should the time and resources best be used in terms of getting to young people and encourage them not to drink?

Mr. Newton. That's a very good question, Mr. Keller. I think we need a comprehensive educational approach in all grade levels. I do believe it needs to start in elementary, and it continues through middle school and high school.

I think because the kids that I'm concerned about the most are the 6 million that I mentioned that come from a family where there's a drinking problem or another drug problem already established in the family, I would like to provide early education for those kids and help them cope with that type of family system, because there's a lot of research in any case that is a very emotional turmoil for a young person living in that type of family.

So I think we need a comprehensive approach through all grade levels, K through 12. And that would be my hope if there was a Federal strategy to implement that type of comprehensive approach.

Mr. Keller. Thank you. Mrs. Katz, what's your opinion on the education aspect, and what ages should we focus a lot of our time and resources?

Mrs. Katz. Our Family Talk About Drinking program was created by an advisory panel of people in alcohol prevention, alcohol treatment, education, and family counseling, and they recommend that you start the discussion with your children when they're quite young, as young as eight.

Now when they're that age, it's a very general discussion, but as they get older, the discussion becomes much more pointed, and it's an ongoing dialog. And when I say a discussion I mean more than just a conversation. As your teens get to 15, 16, 17 years old, you need to start really becoming an active part of their life, much the same way you had to when they were babies.

In fact, the adolescent years are somewhat like a rebirth, and kids need in their teen years as much time and attention from their parents as they did when they were newborns. And that means that you know who their friends are. You know who their friends' parents are, and you make sure that they share your same values. You know where they're going on a Friday or Saturday night, and you're awake when they get home. And thanks to the advent of cell phones, hopefully while they're out, you even keep track of them, you know, as well. And I know that's what I do as a mom.

Mr. Keller. Thank you. And, Coach, I'll yield back.

Mr. Osborne. Thank you, Mr. Keller.

Mr. Case?

Mr. Case. Thank you, Mr. Chair. I share my Ranking Member's welcome acceptance of your initiative in this area.

Let me ask a bullet question of each of you in my 5 minutes, so that means 1 minute each. What should the Federal Government do to combat underage drinking at this point? I think we've diagnosed the problem pretty well. It seems to me that the options are regulatory action by our Federal executive branch, funding by our executive and legislative branches, or statutory changes of one kind or another by both branches as well.

So let me just walk down the panel and just give it to me straight and bullet-wise. Ms. Molinari?

Ms. Molinari. Well, I think first of all, it's national leaders I think holding hearings like this and being the influence developers that you are throughout this nation certainly speaking on these issues and employing our programs, any one of the programs that are presented here today to help educate and influence is an important role that you can all play.

Certainly I'd say that we embrace almost the majority of the NAS studies that—the NAS study recommendations that urge the Federal Government to get more involved and wage media campaigns, bring together independent advisory boards such as we do to constantly keep this as a top priority for our nation's leaders.

And certainly in any way, shape or form, Congressman, that we can be of assistance, we'd be very pleased to help you in that.

But as we talk, there is a role—the numbers are still too high—and there's a role for industry, for government, for not-for-profits all likes to play in reducing and saving lives.

Mr. Case. Mr. Newton?

Mr. Newton. Thank you, Mr. Case. I agree with the NSA support recommendations to have a Federal strategy to oversee prevention, intervention and treatment process through communities, schools and throughout our society. I really believe that's the kind of intervention we need by the government right now.

And I do believe that the media campaign would be a huge tool for us to combat the mixed messages for young kids.

Mr. Case. Thank you.

Mrs. Hamilton?

Mrs. Hamilton. Thank you. It's all right here in the NAS report.

This Committee hearing was on what works. Of all of the research that was submitted, nothing that was submitted by the alcohol industry was scientifically evaluated as a science-based program except for Alcohol 101, and that needed further research.

This is a graph from Monitoring the Future that goes from 1975 to 2002. The middle line here where the 21 minimum drinking age changed is where the line goes down. From 1991, it flatlines. All of the programs that have been presented shown that this is not working. You cannot just provide information without having science behind it that proves that it works, and I would urge this Committee to please look at funding for science-based programs that can be scientifically evaluated for this critical public health and safety issue. It's imperative that we look at this.

You know, I really appreciate the ad. I really do. But I have to say that that's only one of 179 that kids see that talk about underage drinking. Kids see 2,400 alcohol ads, or people do, about drunk driving and underage drinking, and they see 209,000 product ads.

We need to have more responsibility from the alcohol industry that talks about what alcohol is. It's for adults.

Mr. Case. OK. Thank you. Let me just keep going. Ms. Hackett?

Federal Government action.

Ms. Hackett. We agree very much with what Mrs. Hamilton said, especially in regards to the National Academy of Sciences report. The Department of Education could also get involved. In Vermont, for example, the Department of Education uses its SADD chapters in its high schools throughout the state to host leadership training, highway safety messaging, substance abuse prevention programs and other positive decision making messages are sent.

The Vermont SADD chapters are a very important part of their statewide community coalition, which is exactly the model that the NAS report states.

Mr. Case. Thank you. Mrs. Katz?

Mrs. Katz. Yes, Congressman. First I have to say that we truly believe that parents play the greatest role here in helping their youth make good decisions. And of course youth see beer advertising in their lives. It's part of society. They may notice an ad.

They may even laugh at an ad or be able to recite something that becomes part of popular culture. But the truth of the matter is that our job as adults is not to pretend that adult things don't exist. It's to help youth navigate through an adult world, and that's where we need to place our efforts.

And in this regard, my company's advertising has tripled since 1982.

Mr. Case. OK. Just briefly, should the Federal Government do anything?

Mrs. Katz. Well, I think the notion that this topic is being ignored is wrong. I think that there's a study that was done by the Fiscal Planning Services of Bethesda, Maryland that said in the year 2000, $8.1 billion was spent by state and Federal Government agencies and private foundations on alcohol-related activities such as alcohol abuse treatment, prevention, education and research.

And I would say that contrary to maybe the answer to a lot of questions, the answer here is not to throw money at it. It's to get parents actively involved in their children's lives. That's what kids have told us is the most important influence, and that doesn't cost anything.

Mr. Case. OK. So is the answer no, we shouldn't do anything?

Or we should continue the Federal Government programs?

Mrs. Katz. I think the Federal Government, state government is already heavily involved in this issue, I would urge them to continue those efforts. And I think my industry and my company has deserved a seat at the table and can play a meaningful role.

Mr. Case. Thank you. Thanks.

Mr. Osborne. Thank you, Mr. Case. Mr. Kind.

Mr. Kind. Thank you, Mr. Chairman. I want to thank our distinguished panelists for your testimony here today. Ms. Molinari, as always, it's a pleasure. And Ms. Hackett, I just want to commend you. You've been extremely poised in testifying. I assume this is your first opportunity to testify before a congressional committee.

You've really done an outstanding job, and I think your representation for students across the country is outstanding in today's panel.

And Mr. Chairman, I want to commend you, too, for highlighting this issue. I think it is an important issue, one that the Committee should take a little more time studying, obviously, with the National Academy of Science report that has come out. As an old college football player myself, I, too, am not insensitive to the messages that the youth and collegiate athletics are subjected to on a daily basis.

And what I see in the state of Wisconsin is a coordinated and comprehensive approach right now to educate our youth, to educate the parents, between beer producers that exist in the state, the beer distributors, to the schools, the Tavern League has a very comprehensive approach, too, and we're starting to see some very fine data coming back in regards to the success of many of these programs.

And I'd hope as we move forward that there will be that type of interest in greater collaboration, greater communication between the various groups that have an interest in trying to reduce underage drinking in this country.

I notice, Mrs. Katz, that Anheuser-Busch has been very aggressive on this front as far as outreach efforts, educating parents in their role in establishing that important communication with their children in the family, working with the retailers in order to try to intercept the underage purchases of alcohol, but also the education efforts with students and youth in particular. Do you have any statistics in regards to the success of the type of programs that Anheuser-Busch has been involved with? Any type of research that's gone on with the approaches that you have taken that you can share with the Committee?

Mrs. Katz. Well, Congressman, the FTC in its 2003 report on youth advertising and underage drinking—I'm sorry. On advertising and underage drinking, rather, commended the industry's educational program, said that they were based on sound research and that they were prepared by people from the educational field, the medical field, the prevention field, and they encouraged the industry to continue those efforts.

If I may, I left half of what I wanted to say to a point that was raised earlier by Congressman Case. If I could just finish. I said that our company's advertising expenditures had tripled since 1982, but teen drinking has gone down 32 percent in that same time period, and teen drunk driving has declined 61 percent.

Now we believe that parents play the greatest role again in addressing this issue, but it also involves retailers, and that's why we put so much emphasis at the point of purchase and encourage retailers to get involved. One of the training programs that we support at the retail level is called TIPS. It stands for Training for Intervention Procedures by Servers of alcohol. And it was created by the founding director of the National Institute on Alcohol Abuse and Alcoholism, Dr. Morris Chafetz, and it has been researched at Virginia Polytechnic and found to be very effective. That's a program that we have wholeheartedly supported for many years, I believe over 20 years.

Mr. Kind. Ms. Katz, do you feel that the beer industry is in a position or willing to try to work with some of the other outside groups and organizations that obviously have an interest, have a lot of ideas that they bring to the table on what approach to take, or do you feel that you're being kind of excluded in the overall discussion of what approach is necessary?

Mrs. Katz. Well, Congressman, I won't comment on whether or not I feel as if we're being excluded, but I will agree that we have a role to play and that it would be wonderful if the outcome of this hearing is that we all remember what the true enemy here is and what we're truly fighting, and that's underage drinking and not each other. And we would hope that this hearing opens the door for more collaboration on the things that we can agree on.

And I'm familiar with some of the programs that Mothers Against Drunk Driving has developed. One that I haven't seen but I've read a press release about is called Alcohol EDU, and it's for high school students, and it emphasizes, according to Mrs. Hamilton, that youth should not drink before they're of legal drinking age, that they should never drink and drive, and that they should never get in the car with anyone who's been drinking.

Those are messages that we not only wholeheartedly support, those are the very same messages that we're conveying in our programs. So my hope is that we can work together on areas where we have common ground and remember what our true aim here is, and that is to continue the progress in the fight against underage drinking.

Mr. Kind. Thank you. And Ms. Hackett, may I ask you a question? Obviously peer pressure, and we heard from Mr. Newton the role that peer pressure played in his early age in that, but that has a huge role in underage drinking as well. Have you noticed or have you been involved in any programs dealing with peer pressure and educating students on how to deal with the powerful influence of their peers in making these type of societal decisions?

Ms. Hackett. I think that's a large initiative of SADD, is to help create an environment where high school students can go and be in a safe haven, you know, somewhere where they're not going to be pressured by people to drink or to go to parties where people will be drinking, but it gives them an alternative without excluding them from friends.

Mr. Kind. All right. Thank you. Thank you all again, and thank you, Mr. Chairman, for holding this hearing today.

Mr. Osborne. Thank you, Mr. Kind.

Mr. Wilson.

Mr. Wilson. Thank you, Mr. Chairman. And Mr. Chairman, I'd like to thank you for your efforts in having this hearing today. As the father of four children, I have a special interest in this, and also I'm very pleased that when I served in the state senate of South Carolina that I worked very closely with MADD. I have been a member. I don't know if my dues are current to date, but I have been a—and particularly Mr. Bill Rowe of Bluffton, South Carolina, who has been our leader there in South Carolina, is very good about educating persons on the state level, and I'm very grateful.

Please come by and visit my office. Ms. Hackett would like this, too, but I've got a—

Mrs. Hamilton. I'll be in South Carolina next week.

Mr. Wilson. Oh, wonderful. Hey, that's terrific. I've got a certificate of merit on the wall. And so thank you. You make a real difference on the state level, both of you, MADD and SADD.

Additionally, I want to submit a statement for the record, and I want to commend the beer wholesalers. I've worked with them over the years, in particular Larry Lipoff of Charleston, with the Pearlstein Distributors in Ridgeland, South Carolina, and they have an extraordinary program. This is a very depressed community. And they have a program that's real life of working with firefighters and with police officers to explain the consequences of driving intoxicated.

Additionally, in Orangeburg, South Carolina, I have known multiple generations of the Barudi family. Murray Barudi, Orangeburg Distributors. He actually recruited Hootie and the Blowfish to provide a little video to warn against young people drinking and the consequences. And it's been seen and reached 142 million people.

But I've got this statement for the record.

And at this time, in the interest of time, Ms. Hackett, I was very interested in your point about having mentoring, because I believe that peer pressure has been indicated with Mr. Newton too that mentoring can be very helpful. Can you tell us of any examples in your experience of mentoring?

Ms. Hackett. Each SADD chapter focuses on mentoring in a different way, but my particular chapter, we do DARE role modeling, where we'll go into elementary schools with DARE officers near the end of their curriculum, and take questions from the students about what it's like to be asked to use, if we've ever been asked.

We also have a program called the Just Say No Traveling Show where our members who signed the pledge to be no use will go into middle schools and elementary schools, not just in our district, but around the state. And they perform skits about prevention, underage drinking and violence.

Mr. Wilson. And I was particularly happy to hear about the Just Say No. To me, that program is so positive, and it's a positive negative message. And so thank you for even referencing that.

And Congresswoman Molinari, it's wonderful to have you back.

And particularly your work with the Century Council, it makes a difference. And you've indicated that research has shown that parents are the most influential factor in an adolescent's decision to drink or not. Could you please explain any initiatives that you may have that emphasizes that point?

Ms. Molinari. Yes sir. I think we all certainly agree here that there's so much—there's a role for all of us to play—government, industry, not-for-profit organizations, as we are too, but that to Francine's point, we can't—you want data. The data states time and time again that the most important influence in a person's ability, a young person's ability to choose to drink or not, comes from their parents.

And let me just cite one more study that we did through Teenage Research Unlimited several years ago. We interviewed over 2,000 teenagers, and then we interviewed the same amount of parents of teenagers. Seventy percent of the parents believed in the last 3 weeks they had a meaningful conversation about underage drinking with their teenager. Seventy percent of the teenagers said they had not talked to their parents about underage drinking yet.

So a lot of what our programs aim to do is to say if you're talking, they're not hearing you or you're talking through each other.

So our programs like You're Not Done Yet and a lot of our other programs go directly to the parents, and most particularly the program that we're gearing right now for 10-year-olds and up will be directed through middle schools but primarily the message will be geared toward the parents, which will be a facilitator's guide and also a message in conjunction with a television, positive television representative personality, which I can't name yet, but one that you'll all think is a good thing, to help communicate to parents and very young people about the dangers of underage drinking.

It's a message that needs to be reinforced to parents, a consequence and a level. There's the right way and the wrong—there's the really right way for parents to communicate with their children about underage drinking, but I don't think there's a wrong way.

The conversation just has to take place.

Mr. Wilson. Thank you. We appreciate your service and your husband's service, too.

Ms. Molinari. Thank you.

Mr. Wilson. And Mrs. Katz, you've indicated that Anheuser-Busch has programs in place to promote greater parent-child communication. And that's the key as identified by the other persons here today. Can you restate those real quickly in the interest of time?

Mrs. Katz. The programs that we have are aimed at parents of young children, Family Talk About Drinking, which helps parents initiate the conversation with their children. As those children move into their teenage years and are heading off to college, we have another program called College Talk, and that program helps parents help their teens continue to make good decisions as they head out of the home and to college.

And then finally, we are an avid supporter of mentoring programs for those students who don't have that kind of strong parental influence at home.

But I'd just like to make one comment if I may about the Roper Research organization's poll of young people, because actually that poll asks youth to identify their influences on a whole host of topics—music, what clothes they wear. Whether or not they're going to drink is one of the answers, or one of the questions, rather. And when it comes to things like music and what clothes they wear, parents don't really play a role.

But when it comes to important decisions in their lives like whether or not they're going to drink or what they're going to be when they grow up, they look to their parents. And advertising has always been one of the choices on this survey, and it has always ranked dead last.

And we believe that if youth have so firmly told us that their parents are such an important factor in this decision, they don't want their parents' disapproval, they want to do the right thing, if 82 percent of today's teens are not drinking, let's continue to use what works. I agree that we are far away from claiming victory.

There are still far too many teens who drink. But we're on the right track. And we need to reinforce that there's progress that's been made. Because if we don't, we lose the opportunity to help students understand that their efforts are working.

I applaud the work that SADD does. In fact, Anheuser-Busch was a founding corporate sponsor of SADD. And my older daughter was a member of SADD when she was in high school. It's a wonderful program, and it complements what parents should be doing at home, and it helps youth make good decisions. And in the end, that's what this comes down to.

Mr. Wilson. Thank you all for being here today. Thank you, Mr. Chairman.

[The prepared statement of Mr. Wilson follows:]

Statement of Hon. Joe Wilson, a Representative in Congress from the State of South Carolina

Thank you, Mr. Chairman for convening this hearing on what works in the fight against illegal underage consumption of alcohol. I commend you for focusing on the solutions rather than the problem itself. We all know great strides have been made in the last twenty years; however, there is more to be done. Parents, schools, communities, and the industry must band together to identify what works in our communities and do more.

Early intervention by parents, schools, and community partners is paramount in taking this fight to the battlefields where it is fought. As the father of four children, I have long supported community efforts to prevent underage drinking. In the state Senate I received Mothers Against Drunk

Driving's (MADD's) Certificate of Merit award, and proudly display that award in my Congressional office.

I want to speak about what works in my community. In the district I represent, and across South Carolina, beer wholesalers have exemplified a strong dedication in their communities in the fight against illegal underage consumption. There are more underage drinking prevention programs at work in South Carolina's Second District , and nationwide, than we have time to enumerate here today, but I want to tell you about just a few. Additionally, because I believe in the MADD program, I have been a member led by Bill Roe of Bluffta, SC.

In Ridgeland, South Carolina, Pearlstine Distributors, led by President Larry Lipor of Charleston, hosts a program called "Street Smart," which uses firefighters and paramedics to present high school and middle school students with a real-life look at the consequences of underage drinking.

Additionally, Orangeburg Distributors is an industry leader in the fight against illegal underage consumption. Orangeburg Distributors President, Murray Baroody, enlisted the help of his friends, pop musicians "Hootie and the Blowfish," to record a Public Service Announcement which has reached more than 142 million people.

Orangeburg has a continuous rotation of underage drinking prevention outdoor ads, radio spots and print ads, and Orangeburg recently sponsored a talk by emergency room nurse Linda Dutil, who makes a dramatic presentation showing students the harmful effects of binge drinking and drunk driving accidents.

Both of these operations participate in the "WE ID" program that offers retailers ID training and a variety of materials, from buttons to stickers for cooler doors and store entrances.

Across the state, the industry works with local high schools to promote safe and fun celebrations for seniors on graduation or prom nights—by providing food, games, entertainment, and a Zero Tolerance for alcohol.

Again, the efforts that I have touched on today highlight just a few of the important and successful programs being implemented by beer wholesalers in my district and state. I urge my colleagues to allow for full consideration of the industry's commitment to this important issue and its efforts to address our mutual concerns.

Mr. Chairman, again I would like to thank you for your efforts in preventing underage consumption by having this hearing today. I am confident that we are all here to reach the same goal, though we may have different ways of going about it.

I look forward to working with my colleagues as well as all the public and private entities to find a solution to the underage drinking situation that is facing our children and American families.

Mr. Osborne. Thank you, Mr. Wilson.

Mr. Davis.

Mr. Davis. Thank you very much, Mr. Chairman. And let me commend you for helping to make sure that this issue gets raised.

As one who has spent much of my adult life working with young people and members of my family working with young people as teachers and principals and Boy Scouts and Girl Scouts and Sun-day school and the whole works, I think it's a very relevant discussion.

As I listen to the different type programs and the different activities that seem to work, it occurs to me that I represent a district that has a large disadvantaged area, large disadvantaged population. Many families are dysfunctional. And so the normalcy of family impact and family influence oftentimes does not occur, or it occurs in a very different kind of way.

My question, Mrs. Katz, is really to you. You've put a lot of emphasis on parent or parental influence on decisions and behavior of children. Do you have programs that work most directly with organizations and groups—I mean, I find that interaction, local community groups, local community organizations, seem to have a greater opportunity to reach not only teenagers or young people, but in many instances, their parents as well. And so television messages, ads, don't seem to work as well in some of these areas as the direct interaction. And so my question is, do you have programs that promote that kind of direct interaction and involvement with communities?

Mrs. Katz. Absolutely, Congressman Davis. In fact, our wholesalers, who are in virtually every community across the country, bring the programs that I've referenced today to their communities, and they work with local organizations to get them implemented.

Nationally, we've worked with many organizations to get these programs into the hands of parents or to bring speakers into schools. Those that we've worked with include some of our states attorneys general, the National Collegiate Athletic Association Foundation, the University of Virginia, Florida State University.

We have worked with Boys and Girls Clubs.

We've worked with organizations throughout the country, because we believe that, again, while it's so important for parents to play a meaningful role in their lives, a group like the Jaycees or the Junior League can help us get these materials to parents and help start those discussions, and that's the most important thing.

So, yes, we work with community organizations throughout the country.

Mr. Davis. And I would encourage you to even do more outreach, for example, while many of the groups that you just mentioned in parts of what would be my congressional district, because I represent downtown Chicago and everything in it, but I also represent other areas where the organizations, for example, that you just mentioned, would not be a part of those communities. And so I would encourage some additional outreach to groups that perhaps are not as traditional, not as well known, but are in fact emerging as part of the decision making process.

And the only other comment that I'd have, I want to commend MADD. I've been a great fan of MADD since its inception from day one, SADD, any groups that are really working, because I think that people learn what they live. And I do believe that there are opportunities to influence behavior and that as individuals learn, then they will apply what they know to daily living and make decisions in a different way.

And so I thank you very much. And thank you, Mr. Chairman.

Ms. Molinari. Congressman? Could I—when we have a conversation about how the Federal Government can get involved, I'd like to ask, because your point is well taken, and very similar programs are run by the Distilled Spirits, through the Boys and Girls Clubs, through the NCAA, through colleges and high schools. But certainly you are all—are grassroots in many ways, and if there are organizations to any of you that you think we can work—and I'll speak for the beer industry too—we'd all be happy to hear of your suggestions as to where we can take our programs or help you if you can help us facilitate relationships to get into those venues, we'd be more than happy to pursue those and would consider it an honor to work with you in the future.

Mr. Davis. I'd be very pleased to do that.

Ms. Molinari. Terrific. Thank you.

Mr. Davis. And we will make it a point. Because I work with a group called Prevention Partnership that does outstanding work.

And I know that they, as well as others, would be interested.

Ms. Molinari. Terrific. We would welcome the opportunity, as well.

Mr. Davis. Thank you very much.

Mrs. Hamilton. Mr. Vice Chairman, could I just mention a few more things? I really want to thank this Committee for taking the opportunity to look at this issue very carefully, but I also—

Mr. Osborne. Would you hold off just a second?

Mrs. Hamilton. I apologize.

Mr. Osborne. We have one more member who has some questions, and so thank you, Mr. Davis. And Mrs. Davis?

Mrs. Davis. Thank you, Mr. Chairman, and I'm sorry that I missed your earlier testimony. You may have spoken about this, but if I can ask a little bit more about what is research-based to you? What does that entail, and how do we go about that?

Mrs. Hamilton. Research-based is independently evaluated.

When MADD's Protecting You Protecting Me program, which is a curriculum for first through fifth graders, was named as a model program by the Federal Government, it went through a rigorous process to get on the national registry of effective programs. It has to go to at least three separate independent evaluating organizations to look at. There's a criteria that they grade upon, and it has to meet that criteria. Everybody has to agree on it in order to get on it. Of the over 700 programs that were submitted for evaluation, I believe there are only about 50 that were named as a model program.

So it's important that independent people look at the program that has been put before them, that they look at the science behind to see if those programs were developed based on science and shown to work to change behavior and to make a difference.

Mrs. Davis. In your estimate, is that what's happening across the board?

Mrs. Hamilton. Unfortunately, no. And that's what we're very, very concerned about, is that the programs that were shown to the NAS is that they were not scientifically evaluated, and we're talking about using Federal funds in the school system to talk about underage drinking programs.

We want to emphasize that these programs that are used within the school system that are getting taxpayer-funded need to be scientifically evaluated by independent researchers and shown to work.

Mrs. Davis. One of my other concerns is the extent to which the young people are included in that. And perhaps, Ms. Hackett, you can respond to that. Because I know in the state of California, for example, there was a time when we spent a lot of money trying to reach young couples on unwed pregnancy. And in fact, you know, young people sat and watched the commercials and the spot, you know, they responded flatly to them. They really didn't speak to them. They didn't speak to what would change their behavior.

And so I'm wondering the extent to which we've really been able to get at the heart of that, and obviously for different groups, for different ages, but how much effort goes into really engaging young people in doing their own ads, what is it that would speak to them particularly? Obviously using rock stars and people that they care about make a difference. But I'm trying to get a sense of how much of that is really going on, and are we asking those questions about the response of young people?

Mr. Newton. You know, real quick, Mrs. Davis, I think it's hard to scientifically evaluate human behavior. I think, you know, a lot of times these intervention and prevention programs affect each young person differently at a different time. But if they don't have the information available, that's what hurts the most.

With all due respect, I think the efforts by the alcohol industry in this regard is—and the money spent and the programs developed—is a minute effort compared to the promotion of alcohol. So I would like the excise tax, if that was passed, that those funds would be totally facilitated through the government, and the alcohol industry wouldn't have any choice of how that money is used.

Thank you.

Mrs. Katz. If I may, Mrs. Hamilton referred to the drug-free schools money and the fact that taxpayer funding goes to pay for these programs. I understand that MADD's programs are at a cost to the school, but all of our programs are free of charge. We pay for them. Our wholesalers bring speakers to schools free of charge.

So there is no taxpayer cost.

And I strongly believe that, as Susan Molinari said, that when you have a speaker addressing high school students, in our instance we have about, I believe, ten speakers, one of whom is the cause of a drunk driving accident. He was the driver, and he killed his younger brother. When you have somebody like that telling his story to young people, I think it's very powerful. He's come to my daughter's school. He's spoken to her peers, and it has a very powerful effect.

And I'm not sure that you can gauge that on a scale. I can tell you that we get many, many letters commending these kinds of programs from young people, saying that they're making a difference. A family talk about drinking program. We actually independently go out and have people evaluate the families that have gotten the materials to see whether they think the materials were helpful, and we've received positive responses.

So we believe we're on the right track. But I hope the effort here is not to exclude some programs and say that some are better than others or only certain people should be at the table. My company has invested with our wholesalers nearly half a billion dollars in these efforts, and our commitment is sincere. And we believe that we can be and should be part of the solution.

Mrs. Hamilton. I'm not saying that they should be excluded.

What I'm saying is that the taxpayer money should be spent on programs that are scientifically and independently evaluated that show results. That's what I said.

We've got to educate not only our children on this very important issue about underage drinking from the time they get to first grade all the way through high school, every single year we've got to have a constant funding stream that helps these programs continue to work. But we've also got to tell parents and adults in this country the truth about what's going on with underage drinking, because they do not know. They do not understand what a child's developing brain looks like when it's been—when they're using alcohol regularly. They don't understand that the frontal lobes and the hippocampus are being affected by underage drinking. Adults do not know that.

We've got to have an adult-focused media campaign so that parents start learning this. Mr. Newton talked about that. His dad was an alcoholic. Children in this country are growing up in families where alcohol is not used responsibly. Those parents don't understand what kind of a message they're sending to their children.

Ms. Davis. Thank you. I was going to ask, Ms. Hackett, if you could respond for a second whether you think that, you know, as adults, do we ask you enough what you think about the effort that's going on?

Ms. Hackett. I think there's a pretty wide gap between what parents think their kids are doing and what their kids are doing.

And that's why I think it's very important that we set a media campaign targeted toward the parents.

We need to inform the parents of what their kids are doing and how to help their kids make the right decisions.

Mrs. Davis. Are adults listening to you?

Ms. Hackett. I think the adults would listen if they were given the right ways, you know. You can affect anyone. We just have to figure out what media campaign we want to use. The example that the Anheuser-Busch showed, their ad that is a prevention ad for underage drinking, isn't being talked about nearly as much as the ones where you see a dog go and bite the groin of a man for the alcohol. So we need to figure out what's targeting who. You know, more of my friends were going in and quoting that commercial than going in and talking about, you know, putting on makeup in the car to go to a convenience store.

Mrs. Davis. And Ms. Molinari?

Ms. Molinari. I just wanted to all say that we have learned over the years of this program, and perhaps the hard way, and while we do use the Federal resources, Department of Education, NIAAA, SAMHSA, in our program development, they have been—NTSB—extremely helpful in helping us develop our educational programs.

When we get to the actual implementation of the programs and how the program looks, we have young people involved now in every stage of it. We go to the younger children in the middle school programs, the college students in our Alcohol 101 Plus, so that at least we design an environment that's reflective of their environment and speak their language so the door stays open as long as possible while we try to get our message through.

Mrs. Davis. I appreciate that. I think we're doing a better job at that. For a long time we weren't.

Mr. Osborne. Thank you, Mrs. Davis. A little role reversal here.

I'd like to defer to the Chairman of the Committee.

Chairman CASTLE. Well, thank you, Mr. Chairman, and thank you, Mr. Newton, for coaching him well to be a good Congressman.

We appreciate it.

[Laughter.]

Chairman Castle. I'm going to talk from my own experience, and I've got to tell you right away up front, this is not scientific and not independent. These are just things I've observed at home and things that I've done that have worked pretty well.

And perhaps this is to Mrs. Hamilton and to Ms. Hackett initially, but it's based—not based on, but Mrs. Katz referred to it as well, and that is the experience of young people testifying, or other people, members of MADD and SADD who I've worked with back as a local official in Delaware, in coming into schools and talking to them, and frankly, showing pictures, showing slides, having that discussion, tears, the whole thing.

That has a galvanizing effect on those young crowds, and I'm talking about high school kids, 9th through 12th grade, say, so you're talking about, you know, 15, 16, 17, 14, 18-year-olds, perhaps. And I'm not sure it's a permanent effect or a lasting effect, but to me of all the things that I saw in dealing with kids when they actually had known somebody or knew of somebody and they saw what had happened, by God, they sat up and paid attention.

Are your two organizations still doing that on a regular basis, or is that sort of not proper anymore? Where does that—where is that on the radar screen?

Mrs. Hamilton. Unfortunately, because we see over 17,000 fatalities and over a half million injuries due to drunk driving every single year in this country, we get a fresh crop of victims who come to MADD to look for our services, and victims who speak on victim impact panels in front of schools and to offenders all across this country are working.

There is no scientific evaluation that shows that—we know that those programs do have an immediate impact on those kids. It is very heart-wrenching to go and listen to that. It's heart-wrenching to do. I've done it many, many times myself. We work with a lot of people whose children have killed themselves in drunk driving crashes, and a lot of people who've driven drunk and killed other people in crashes.

So we're very experienced at working with all kinds of people.

What we don't know is the long-term range effect of whether hearing that at that particular time is going to change somebody's attitudes and behavior way down the line. Of course, we hope that it's making a difference, but there's more research that needs to be done on that.

Chairman Castle. How do you look at it, Ms. Hackett? No research needs to be done in my mind, by the way, but that's all right.

Ms. Hackett. The way that SADD works is each chapter decides what initiatives they want to take that would be the most effective in their school and community environments. And in a lot of cases, schools will do specific programming that will reach their students due to something that has happened in the school of students have been in accidents involving drunk driving.

So SADD really aims to, you know, target the school, help the kids where they need it, and, you know, give them something that they need to hear and something that they can relate to.

Chairman Castle. OK. Well, thank you both for your interest.

Let me go on to another question, and I'm not sure of the answer, so maybe all of you should just answer briefly if you can, and that is, the other thing I've seen that had just a dramatic effect on my friends, among others, and the behavior of people, are the roadblocks for drunk driving.

But with young people, if you've had so much as any alcohol whatsoever, you've got a problem. You're going to lose your license.

So it's not just drunk driving. It's also anybody who is young who is driving. Generally, they're 16. Some may be cheating on that, too. So you're dealing with individuals who can get in a lot of trouble. And in Delaware, we've done quite a bit of radio advertising on that particular subject, which I think has deterred some young people from getting into cars at least, and hopefully they're more thoughtful about it.

I mean, I've seen the effect of it at cocktail parties. People are very careful, because we have quite a few roadblocks in Delaware, and they're very cautious about it. And I've been out there with the police on the roadblocks, and I've seen the reaction of people. They are panicked when this happens, even if they haven't been drinking, they're probably panicked. But they are.

And that also has had—I mean, that has had a dramatic effect on the older population, but also on a younger population. There are some legal questions about it, none of which I think have been really sustained in any courts. First of all, is there any group represented here or that you know of that's opposed to that for any legal reasons, or anything of that nature? None of your groups are—

Mrs. Hamilton. Opposed to sobriety checkpoints?

Chairman Castle. Opposed to sobriety checkpoints.

Mrs. Hamilton. No.

Mrs. Katz. Well, we are adamantly opposed to drunk driving, and to the effective measures that can address drunk driving, we are wholehearted supporters. When it comes to teens, for over a decade we have supported an initiative called graduated licensing that helps youth get graduated privileges so that they ease into the driving privilege and they don't from 16 years old get full driving privileges.

But I know that most youth who die in automobile crashes die in non-alcohol-related fatalities. And so that is the No. 1 leading cause of death among youth, and we also need to get a message out to young people about not wearing their seat belts, and driving too quickly.

Chairman Castle. I agree with all that, obviously. And I couldn't agree with you more. But we're focused on the alcohol, really, today and the usage of it. Have any of you seen the effects of it on young people in terms of the sobriety checkpoints or roadblocks?

Mrs. Hamilton. The NAS report also suggests sobriety checkpoints as a deterrent for underage drinking as well as for deterring all impaired driving.

Chairman Castle. So it is recognized by them that there is an underage aspect?

Mrs. Hamilton. Absolutely.

Mr. Newton. I think those checkpoints are a very—can be a very helpful tool to intervene on someone that has a problem. Because it's been shown that legal consequences to drunk driving or to drinking problems, people respond to that because they're forced to, and it helps people get well.

I was a little concerned about the message that was mentioned earlier I think by Mr. Miller about people giving people rides home that are drunk. With underage drinkers, that's kind of can be a mixed message. It's OK to drink as long as you don't drive. It's still an illegal activity. And a lot of those kids will drive if they drink enough. At some point, they will not be able to make a decision not to ask somebody for a ride, and they will get in their car and be a danger.

Ms. Molinari. Well, to that point, one of the programs that we work with local distributors, retailers, police officers, is to try and intervene before we get to that point, and that is the Cops in Shops programs or the point of sale, where we try and use almost that same fear factor, embarrassment factor to say don't even try and buy it if you're under 21, because you know what? You're not just going to get slapped on the wrist anymore in this area. You're going to get—potentially you can get arrested. Potentially, you can never get a driver's license if you continue this behavior. And you know what? That police officer is going to take you home and stare your parents down face to face.

So we also like to see a lot of the intervention take place earlier and the embarrassment so that we don't even get to that point.

Chairman Castle. Well, my time is up, and I don't think, Mr. Chairman, that, you know, fear and intimidation is—obviously education and parental involvement is also extraordinarily important as well as other things, but I do think because alcohol usage is basically viewed as something pleasurable from an early age on. We see it, unfortunately, on television advertising. We see it because adults drink and that kind of thing, that a little bit of fear and deterrence is in order, quite frankly, done legally and done properly.

And I think that has to be part of the agenda of any programs that we put together as we try to deal with this problem.

So we need to get a balance of various things. I appreciate your commenting on your views on those points. I yield back, sir.

Mr. Osborne. Thank you, Mr. Chairman. I think Mr. Case had a comment that he wanted to make before he had to leave.

Mr. Case. Thank you very much, Mr. Chair, and again, I thank you on behalf of my colleagues for holding this hearing. I thank the witnesses. It was a good, balanced panel. We heard from a lot of different perspectives.

I think we could probably sit here for another couple of hours.

I certainly could. We didn't even touch some issues that frankly we should have gotten into.

Just a couple of observations. First of all, from my own personal perspective, and I believe I speak for several of my colleagues, I don't think that the answers here are going to lie outside of Federal Government action exclusively. I don't believe that we can pull this off by simply deferring to the industry and to the schools and to the states. We are going to need coordinated efforts across the board.

We clearly have a continuing problem. I believe it's getting worse. Perhaps some of the statistics show some positive developments, but overall, I think the pattern is pretty clear; that we are exposing our youth to alcohol on a much more regular basis, and they are in fact consuming alcohol on a much more regular basis, and something is not working.

Now I think we would all agree that one part of the Federal Government's efforts should be devoted to funding prevention. That is a legitimate thing for us to do collectively. So one place we can certainly start is with the zeroing out of the $30 million in the current President's budget.

One of my colleagues made the comment earlier that there are going to be some casualties of balancing a budget deficit that's worsening every day. I totally agree with that. I just don't think this should be the casualty. I don't think that this is the right message at all. We've been talking about messages the whole day. And the message that the Federal Government doesn't believe that alcohol prevention in K to 12 is important is the wrong message.

Second, we have not talked yet about advertising sufficiently, I don't believe. Certainly what bothers me as one member is the low percentage devoted by the alcohol industry to so-called responsibility advertising. I'm not sure that looking out over the—fairly over the entire scene we can assume, nor should we ask of the alcohol industry to fund perhaps a much higher level perhaps where we'd all like to see it, like 50 percent or something like that. So it seems to me that we've got to think of some form of getting a lot more of that responsibility advertising out over the airwaves both to adults—and I agree that adults have to be very much the focus—but also to teen drinking. I don't think it's going to be enough for adults.

The comment by Mr. Davis that we can't just simply focus on families, when so much of the problem in our country is a breakdown in families—where families are not effectively delivering messages, means that we have to find other ways of reaching children who are not going to be reached through their families, and oftentimes that is—and by the way, not only through schools either.

Sometimes those teens are operating outside of the normal school environment. So, clearly, it has to be advertising at some point, it seems to me.

And I do believe finally that the alcohol industry should very much be at the table, that they need to be a part of the discussion, that we all need to be at the table together. So to you, Mrs. Katz, you said it to me twice, and I heard it—I heard you say it one more time, so obviously there's some sensitivity there. I believe that you should be there.

But the bottom line is that to leave this unaddressed or to leave this to the current kind of approach, which is some level of minimal effort by the Federal Government, a tremendous amount of effort by community organizations such as MADD, SADD, recovering alcoholics such as you, thank you very much for being here and telling us your story, and to voluntary appearances by people who have suffered, and to basically trust in an industry which is still devoted No. 1 to the marketing and increased consumption of its product, seems to me to be unrealistic.

So I hope that we would all be able to support a collective effort, probably through our Federal Government.

Thank you.

Mr. Osborne. Thank you, Mr. Case. I would just like to make a couple of closing comments, and then we'll let you get on your way. You've been sitting here a long time. You've been very patient and articulate, and we appreciate your attendance today.

The reason that I wanted to have this hearing was that the National Academy of Science spent a lot of time on this report. They are an independent, outside, scientifically based agency. And so we didn't want their recommendations just to go unheard or forgotten.

So often, that's what happens. The Federal Government says, well, you guys go study it. They produce a report, and then it stays on a shelf somewhere, nobody pays any attention.

And I think we've got to pay attention to this, because when you look at the fact that 25 percent of our eighth graders are drunk every month, those are the kids that are coming up. They're 13 and 14 years old. And we've said over and over again here today, that's a whole different deal than somebody 21 or 22 getting drunk. And so to say that the problem's going away, or it isn't much of a problem, I don't think is really very accurate.

Obviously, when the drinking age was raised to 21, we saw a pretty steep drop. As has been mentioned, since then, it really hasn't declined much. And so what the National Academy of Science said, No. 1, they think we ought to have a federally funded program that's aimed at parents. And I would agree with that, because I think as Ms. Hackett said, there's a tremendous gap between what parents think is happening and what is really happening. They don't have a clue, most of them.

But also, Danny Davis made a good point. We've got 20 million fatherless kids in this country. We have a huge number of kids who don't have a parent they can turn to. We have a lot of parents, as Bob mentioned, that are currently alcohol-dependent, and you can't count on one of those parents to be a very good adviser to their children. So certainly we've got to aim at the parents, but we've got a $53 billion problem here.

Second recommendation was that the alcohol industry refrain from marketing practices that appeal to youth. And I really appreciate Mrs. Katz being here and what she had to say, and also Ms.

Molinari. I think you both represent your industries very well and made some very good points. But I think most people would have to say that maybe the overwhelming majority of what kids see is not the ad don't drink, but they see young people having a good time. They're athletic, and they sometimes make that connection, that if you're going to have a party, if you win a championship, you've got to have alcohol. And it's there, very prevalent. So that was their second recommendation.

There were 30 million underage kids that saw the Super Bowl, and you say, well, what was the overall message that they got from those Super Bowl ads? Was it pro or anti-underage drinking? Probably many people would say it was more pro.

And then last, we need a Federal coordination and support that the Federal Government is doing a very poor job of coordinating what they do spend. They're not spending enough. And as Mr. Castle and I and others here know, the Federal budget is a real issue right now. I don't know what's going to happen.

But we appreciate your being here today. We appreciate all of you for what steps you have taken to prevent, and I think each one of you here is sincere in what you're doing.

So with that, I will end the hearing. And I'd like to thank the witnesses and members for their valuable time.

If there's no further business, the Subcommittee stands adjourned.

[Whereupon, at 1:32 p.m., the Subcommittee was adjourned.]

[Additional material submitted for the record follows:]

Chapter 4

ADDITIONAL MATERIALS SUPPLIED

LETTER FROM BOB ANASTAS, FOUNDER, STUDENTS AGAINST DRIVING DRUNK, SUBMITTED FOR THE RECORD

The Honorable Mike Castle
Education Reform Committee
House of Representatives
Washington, D.C.

Dear Representative Castle:

I understand that you recently conducted a hearing on underage drinking. As the founder of Students Against Driving Drunk (SADD), now called Students Against Destructive Decisions, I have a long history of working to address this issue.

While we've seen significant progress on preventing underage drinking since I began SADD back in the early 1980s, there is much more work to be done. The creation of SADD came out of my desire to inspire young people to help solve this problem. We all know parents are most important in raising our young people, but when the empowerment message comes from one teen to another, that, too, can have a great impact.

As a high-school hockey coach, I lost two of my students to drunk-driving crashes in the course of a year. And I saw too many other students who were "near misses."

That's what drove me to begin speaking out on this subject and to create SADD and the original "Contract for Life" between parents and teens. Not only did the contract encourage young people to make wise choices like not drinking and not getting into a car with someone who had been drinking, it also encouraged parents to set a good example for their children.

From the beginning of my efforts to found SADD and speak out on this issue, Anheuser–Busch has been a partner in helping me reach students with my prevention message. Over the past 20 years, I have spoken to literally millions of students, and Anheuser–Busch wholesalers across the country have been key in making that happen. Since I began speaking on this subject, I have now expanded my program to include not only a prevention message on teen drinking and drunk driving, but one that encourages teens to reject racism and hatred, while working together to solve societal issues.

If solving underage drinking was easy, we would have conquered it in the 1980s, but it's not. It will take teamwork, including individuals like myself and the beer industry, to continue the progress that's been made. I appreciate the opportunity to share my views on this important issue with you.

Very truly yours,
Bob Anastas
Founder
Students Against Driving Drunk

Letter from Dale & Thomas Baker, PhDs, Family–School–Community Partnerships, Submitted for the Record

Honorable Michael N. Castle, Chairman
Subcommittee on Education Reform
U.S. House of Representatives
Washington, DC 20515

Dear Congressman Castle and other Subcommittee Members:

Like you, we are deeply concerned about the problems created by underage drinking. Alcohol abuse at any age is harmful. Underage drinking is damaging because it prevents healthy development and sidetracks young people from preparation for the future.

The recent National Academy of Sciences report rightfully recognizes the crucial role parents and other adults play in the prevention of underage drinking. Parents are the most important protective factor and a powerful force in halting the use of alcohol by young people. Parents who clearly and frequently tell their children they do not want them to drink are less likely to have children who drink. Most young people do not want to experience disapproval from their parents nor violate their trust.

Unfortunately, many young people lack guidance from the adults in their lives.

Many parents believe that the consumption of alcohol by adolescents is a right of passage over which they have little control. Other parents are inattentive or distance themselves from their teenage children. Public policy that reinforces the family leadership role of parents is the most effective strategy for the prevention of underage drinking. Mentoring services are essential for those children who are "raising themselves."

Comments from scores of parents attending our "Parenting Your Teenager" work-shops confirm that underage drinking is reduced when they make it clear they expect their kids not to drink. We receive the same feedback during our “Parent University” and our “Responsibility Building Workshop for Parents & Kids” programs.

Our conclusion is that parents need to be reminded and educated regarding their vital role in the prevention of underage drinking.

A useful model in this regard is “Family Talk About Drinking” produced by Anheuser–Busch. This video, available in both English and Spanish, helps parents understand how to explain to their kids that underage drinking is illegal and inappropriate. Parents need to know they are responsible for teaching their kids how to make good decisions. Not all parents understand this obligation. We are pleased to have served on the advisory group during the creation of this video.

“Caring Connections: Helping Young People from Troubled Homes” was also funded by a grant from Anheuser–Busch. The publication suggests practical ways educators can connect with young people who face adversity. One key to understanding why some young people thrive while others fail is the concept of resilience—the capacity to overcome the odds. Big classes and large guidance loads spreads the talents of teachers and counselors impossibly thin. Yet, every student needs the direct encouragement of at least one trustworthy adult at school who reinforces the young person’s resiliency. This suggests the importance of school-based and agency-based programs that train and assign adult mentors. We should mention that while generous in its funding, Anheuser–Busch did not request nor have any control over the content in this publication. Dr. Terrel Bell, President Reagan’s Secretary of Education, was executive editor of the publication. We were the lead writers.

As you consider public policy regarding the prevention of underage drinking, please consider the value of programs that educate parents and guardians regarding their leadership role with their children. Parenting education and mentoring programs are valuable tools in this regard.

Respectfully submitted for your consideration.

Dale & Thomas Baker, PhDs
Family–School–Community Partnerships
A nonprofit organization serving families and youth.

Dale Baker is a clinical psychologist in private practice in La Jolla, CA. Thomas Baker writes parenting education publications and produces videos relating to youth issues.

STATEMENT OF DAVID K. REHR, PHD, PRESIDENT, NATIONAL BEER WHOLESALERS ASSOCIATION

Chairman Castle and members of the Subcommittee, on behalf of the members of the National Beer Wholesalers Association (NBWA) I appreciate the opportunity to submit this testimony in connection with the Subcommittee's hearing on what programs and efforts are effective in helping to reduce and prevent illegal, underage purchase and consumption of licensed beverages. I would also like to thank the Chairman for convening this forum and allowing us the opportunity to share our thoughts on this important topic, provide the committee with an industry perspective and inform its members of just a few of the valuable responsibility programs being implemented nationwide by beer wholesalers.

Industry Programs

Through national, state and local efforts, beer wholesalers and the beer industry in general actively participate in a broad array of highly successful prevention programs that effectively address illegal underage consumption. As a result, the beer industry has become a recognized leader in the fight against illegal underage concerns.

The beer industry has successfully engaged in the effort to reduce illegal underage purchase and consumption. Beer wholesalers have exhibited a genuine commitment to addressing underage concerns and have implemented countless programs in their respective territories and across the nation to communicate a message of legal and responsible consumption of their products. To highlight just a few of the programs, wholesalers currently sponsor identification verification programs at the point-of-sale, retailer education and server training programs, public service announcements, educational speakers in schools, and alcohol-free post prom events. Wholesalers also participate in responsibility messages through advertising and support efforts at the state level for stricter penalties on retailers and consumers engaged in illegal underage purchase and consumption.

Specifically, Golden Eagle Distributors of Tucson, Arizona has implemented a number of youth programs locally. For many years, Golden Eagle has sponsored two unique programs—an essay contest on safety and the "You Auto Buckle Up" seat belt poster contest.

The Golden Eagle Driver's Education Safety Essay Contest is held in area high schools, with one student winner from each high school being awarded a one-year auto insurance policy. The "You Auto Buckle Up" seat belt use poster contest is open to all school levels—elementary through college—with one winner chosen at each level who receives a cash award and is honored at an awards luncheon with their parents. In particular, this program is a good example of involving parents, students, schools and the community in the efforts to address underage concerns.

Another example of proactive wholesaler involvement can be found in El Dorado, Kansas where Demo Sales, Inc. has worked to promote a dialogue between city council members and local licensed beverage retailers. A few years ago the city council voted to establish a Youth Initiative Committee to help deter illegal underage consumption and promote zero tolerance. The group was instrumental in initiating discussions with council members that highlighted retailer concerns and their commitment to preventing illegal underage drinking. Through attendance at city council meetings, the group was invited to propose positive policy initiatives toward the common goal of stopping underage drinking.

Additionally, NBWA members have adopted a Marketing and Communications Code to provide guidance on beer wholesaler marketing and related promotional activities. For example, the NBWA Code states that beer wholesaler promotional activities and marketing should reinforce the legal purchase age. Beer wholesaler marketing is directed to adults of legal purchase age who choose to drink. The Code guides decisions that each wholesale company makes regarding where and how to advertise, promote or make related public statements.

NBWA's Code is further based in principles that are intended to communicate responsibility, legal purchase and consumption, and candor. Specific directives include the avoidance of depicting illegal activity and the avoidance of encouraging or condoning drunk driving, intoxication, or excessive, irresponsible consumption.

NBWA members are committed to abiding by the NBWA Code. We are pleased that these efforts are making a real difference. In fact, illegal purchase and consumption among high school seniors has dropped 30 percent over the last two decades, according to a study sponsored by the National Institute on Drug Abuse. Additionally, thanks to the industry's prevention programs and the efforts of parents, teachers and others, 82% of the nation's youth are now making the right decision to not drink alcohol illegally, according to research from the U.S. Department of Health and Human Services.

Efforts to Account for What Works

Taking into consideration the topic of the hearing–"Preventing Underage Drinking: What Works"–it bears mentioning that Congress has recently taken notice of the fact that there are a myriad of government funded programs at work today and has instructed federal agencies and government panels to inventory the programs.

There have been several attempts to provide some accounting of programs to prevent illegal underage consumption.

As an initial effort, a 2001 General Accounting Office report "Underage Drinking Information on Federal Funds Targeted at Prevention," concluded, among other things, that:

- Twenty-three federal agencies have program efforts that address underage alcohol prevention, and for fiscal year 2000 an estimated $71 million was specifically allocated to efforts designed to reduce underage drinking.
- SAMHSA and approximately 16 other federal agencies identified about $1 billion of fiscal year 2000 combined funding that addressed alcohol prevention and illegal drug use. A breakdown of how that funding was allocated could not be determined.
- An estimated additional $769 million out of $2.2 billion of block, formula and incentive grant funds may have been used by states to address prevention of drug and alcohol use by youth.
- The federal government spends substantial resources on prevention of underage drinking, with no real means of accounting for these resources or the effectiveness of these efforts, questioning the way in which federal agencies are spending taxpayer dollars.

Following up on the GAO report, a comprehensive National Academy of Sciences (NAS) study was mandated in the 2002 Labor, Health and Human Services appropriations bill. This effort, as it was originally stated, was intended as a study of existing federal, state, and non-governmental programs aimed at reducing and preventing illegal underage drinking.

NBWA initially supported Congress's decision to appropriate $500,000 to the National Academy of Sciences to review such programs. The beer wholesaling industry has many successful, effective underage responsibility programs that it was anxious to share with the National Academy.

Regretfully, the National Academy and the advisory committee that was selected to carry out its task missed an opportunity to evaluate programs and failed to follow Congress's mandate, which was to "review existing federal, state, and non-governmental programs, including media-based programs, designed to change the attitudes and health behaviors of youth." Many organizations, including NBWA, submitted documents, articles, videotapes and other materials on a broad range of established responsibility programs designed to address underage issues; however, the

National Academy and the committee ignored outright the industry programs submitted and never removed the materials submitted on approximately 125 wholesaler responsibility programs from their shrink-wrapped packaging.

Time, revenue and resources were expended with the National Academy to determine an adequate accounting of existing programs, their effectiveness and the effective use of taxpayer dollars supporting various programs; however, there is still no answer.

More recently, language was included in the 2004 Omnibus Appropriations bill (P.L. 108–199) to direct the Secretary of HHS to establish an interagency committee on the prevention of illegal underage drinking and issue an annual report summarizing all federal agency activities concerning the issue, issue key surveillance data and progress being made in reducing illegal underage drinking. The Secretary is tasked with taking immediate steps to implement the recommendations of the panel and to prepare a plan for combating underage drinking.

I am encouraged that the Secretary's efforts will allow for progress and also hopeful that this most recent instruction from Congress for an accounting for current programs and an annual progress report comes to fruition. NBWA looks forward to playing a role in this process and stands ready to provide the Secretary with documentation of our members' programs.

Conclusion

The beer industry remains committed to the fight against illegal underage drinking. While real progress has been made, there is more that remains to be done. We must focus on real solutions, such as the programs that are working in our communities, and not untested programs and misguided tax policies. Parents, teachers, community leaders, law enforcement and the industry should continue to work together to keep alcohol out of the hands of our children, and available for adults of legal drinking age to enjoy safely and responsibly. By working together, we can continue to make a difference in the fight against illegal underage drinking.

LETTER FROM DIANE RIIBE, EXECUTIVE DIRECTOR, PROJECT EXTRA MILE, SUBMITTED FOR THE RECORD

The Honorable Thomas Osborne
U.S. House of Representatives
Washington, D.C. 20515–2703

Dear Congressman Osborne:

On behalf of the Project Extra Mile network of community coalitions across Nebraska, thank you for the opportunity to provide input into the hearings in the Education and the Workforce Committee of the House of Representatives set for Wednesday, February 11th. We appreciate this critical review of underage drinking and, in particular, your and Congress' support of the findings of the National Academy of Sciences and Institute of Medicine's report unveiled this past September.

As you may know, Congressman Osborne, Project Extra Mile's community efforts span the state, from Omaha to Scottsbluff. Our efforts began in Omaha in 1995. We know the passion of community folks to create change in their environments regarding underage drinking, to make long-lasting change for generations to come. The challenge is enormous; communities simply cannot do it alone.

We respectfully request that you urge your colleagues to continue a solid funding base for community level environmental prevention activities. We know so many things that work—policy changes at the local and state level; enforcement of youth alcohol laws, ordinances, and school policies; media advocacy around those issues; and education for adults and youth alike—but we need to know that Congress will provide the leadership on a continued basis. Federal funding of underage drinking prevention efforts has been outpaced by virtually every other prevention program, whether it is tobacco prevention or illicit drug use prevention programs. Alcohol use by persons under age 21costs the nation $53 billion each year while thousands of lives are lost in automobile crashes, homicides, suicides, drownings, falls, and other unintentional and intentional injuries.

Schools have a unique opportunity to implement or work for effective strategies with young people and within the community. Some of these include:

- Providing service learning opportunities to connect students with community coalitions to actively engage in changing their environment;
- Enacting effective school alcohol policies that allow for swift and certain response by school officials;
- Restricting alcohol advertisements associated with athletic contests;
- Working with local community leaders, businesses, and others to remove alcohol sponsorship of community events and cultural celebrations;
- Restricting where advertising and promotions are located near schools;
- Working with radio and television stations in the community to restrict alcohol ad placement when youth are a significant portion of the listening or viewing audience.
- Providing media literacy learning opportunities within the curriculum.

We work within Nebraska to bring schools into our community efforts in each of the communities; they are vital partners. Their leadership can effect real change.

Thank you, Congressman Osborne, for looking at some of those ways in which schools can involve themselves within the community to continue their long-standing commitment to the future of children.

Thank you, also, for your perseverance on this issue. Our communities need just such leadership. The result in the future is worth the struggle today. Thank you for bringing our concerns and ideas forward.

Respectfully submitted,
Diane Riibe
Executive Director
Project Extra Mile

Testimony
Hope Taft, First Lady of Ohio
House Subcommittee on Education Reform
"Preventing Underage Drinking - What Works"

February 10, 2004

As the First Lady of Ohio, I thank you for the opportunity to provide testimony to the House Subcommittee on Education Reform to inform the hearing on "Preventing Underage Drinking - What Works." I am one of the 36 current Governors' spouses and 16 Emeritus Members of the Leadership to Keep Children Alcohol Free national initiative. For the past 4 years, I have been the Co-Chair of this unique non-partisan coalition of Governors' spouses, Federal agencies, and public and private organizations. We are devoted to increasing public awareness, engaging policy makers, and mobilizing action to stop childhood drinking. Our specific focus is the 9-15 year-old age group. And we need to focus there. In Ohio, 234 children, aged 6-12, were admitted to a publicly funded treatment program in FY2003. I feel sure Ohio is no different from any other state in this regard.

The brainchild of NIAAA, *Leadership to Keep Children Alcohol Free*, was launched in March 2000 to make childhood drinking prevention a national health priority. In addition to their role as Governors' spouses.

Leadership members are prosecutors, judges, educators, business leaders and parents. Many of us have witnessed through our respective professions or personally, the devastation early alcohol abuse can inflict on individuals, families, our communities, and our Nation.

I speak from my 25 years of experience as a Certified Prevention Specialist, community organizer, and now as First Lady of Ohio. Let me begin by giving you some background on my involvement with this very important public health issue.

In 1986, 1 was approached by Charles Luken, then Mayor of Cincinnati, to help the city develop a prevention strategy for crack cocaine. This effort evolved into Cincinnati's Citizens Against Substance Abuse, a community-based, non-profit, volunteer-driven organization that focused on alcohol, tobacco, and other drug prevention activities and laid the groundwork for Congressman Portman's Coalition for a Drug Free Greater Cincinnati. In 1987, 1 co-founded Ohio Parents for Drug Free Youth. Two years later, I co-founded the Ohio Alcohol and Drug Policy Alliance, a network of statewide education, prevention, treatment, and recovery organizations aimed at effecting policy changes in the alcohol and drug field. As First Lady of Ohio, a key focus of my agenda is the mobilization of Ohio communities to promote positive youth development, with an emphasis on alcohol and illegal drug prevention. As Co-Chair of the Leadership to Keep Children Alcohol Free, I am committed - along with the other Governors' spouses - to carrying the message of die importance of preventing childhood drinking and to challenging parents, policy makers, opinion leaders, the media, and communities to bring about the changes in our Nation's thinking and behavior toward childhood drinking.

We are pleased that the Subcommittee understands the need to address underage drinking and drug use in all its complexity, including early onset of alcohol use by the most vulnerable members of our society - children. We commend you for focusing on Kindergarten to 12th grade, recognizing that while college campuses bear much of the burden of underage drinking problems, the problem certainly doesn't start there.

The magnitude of the problem in middle and high school is staggering - alcohol is the number one drug of choice for kid's 12-20. The graph shows that alcohol use is more prevalent than cigarette or marijuana use in grades 8, 10 and 12. Of even greater concern is that 88% of kids aged 12-20 who consumed alcohol in the month prior to being surveyed reported either binge or heavy drinking, levels that put kids at significant risk. Simultaneously, the age of first alcohol use is dropping.

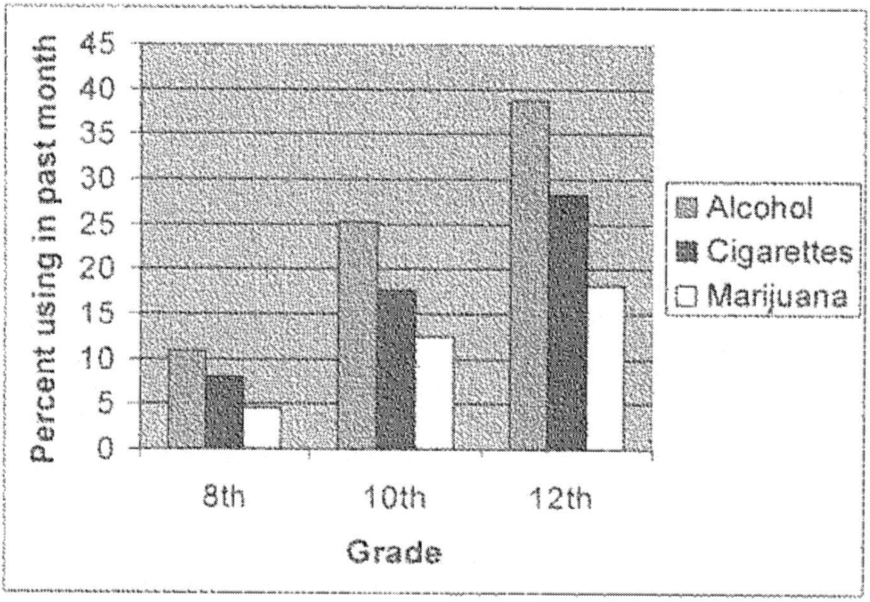

And the risk is not limited to drunk-driving crashes.

Information from research provides us with so much more data than we had even five years ago about the real short-and long-term consequences of alcohol abuse. For example, we now know the impact of early alcohol use upon the brain and how it impairs memory and learning abilities. In addition to the obvious acute consequence of drinking by pre- and early adolescents, ongoing NIAAA research suggests that heavy drinking at this age may set a lifelong trajectory of irreversible consequences. For example, 40% of children who begin drinking before the age of 15 will have alcohol dependence or abuse problems at some point in their lives; adolescents who use alcohol may remember 10% less of what they have learned than those who don't drink; and those who start drinking before age 14 are 12 times more likely to be injured while under the influence of alcohol sometime in their life than those who wait till age 21. Early prevention efforts are imperative!

Let me also dispel an important myth that I have heard repeatedly from parents and from opinion leaders about underage drinking. Some propose that the solution is to adopt the so-called "European model" in which drinking age laws and attitudes are more liberal. The argument is that these policies and attitudes in turn foster more responsible styles of drinking by young people. That is a myth. The "European model" does not work!

In a 1999 survey, conducted with 15 year-olds in 29 European countries, students were asked about drinking to intoxication in the past year. In this comparison, U.S. students are less likely to have been intoxicated in the past year than the majority of their European counterparts. In addition, the World Health Organization report released in

2002 states that one in four deaths among European men aged 15-29 years is alcohol related. This is not the model we should emulate. Governments around the world, including in Europe, are beginning to take action to address underage drinking because of mounting problems.

As I address the question - "what works" - let me offer some overarching truths that I have learned from my 18 years' experience in the prevention field, and from extensive discussions with researchers as a member of several

Federal Advisory Councils. Effective prevention efforts must:

(1) be based on evidence-based principles
(2) address community specific needs;
(3) be SUSTAINED; and
(4) be environmentally oriented so that honest, consistent and age appropriate messages are emphasized in all venues that touch children's lives. Change in community norms, policies, and attitudes must accompany any prevention program so that our children receive consistent messages about the dangers of childhood and adolescent drinking and drug use.

In identifying "what works," schools and communities can rely on the National Institute on Alcohol Abuse and Alcoholism (NIAAA), the Substance Abuse and Mental Health Services Administration (SAMHSA), the Office of Juvenile Justice and Delinquency Prevention (OJJDP), the National Institute on Drug Abuse (NIDA), and the National Highway Traffic Safety Administration (NHTSA) for validated research information, many of these groups have lists of programs that have shown results under rigorous evaluations. But please make sure the Department of Education does not require that a listed program be used.

It makes sense to implement programs that "work", whether for more effective education, reductions in problem behaviors or enhanced employability. Tight budget and common sense demand it. So why not just list all of the programs that "work" and require their implementation. What "works" has be defined as programs that have been proven to be effective using scientific tests with experimental designs.

The problem lies in two areas. First, there are an insufficient number of these "scientifically tested" programs that are both available and feasible to implement. A quick review of the seven most highly publicized lists of "evidence-based programs" reveals that only nine (9) programs are commonly ranked as effective by at least three of these lists. These nine programs include such wide ranging approaches as school based prevention of drug and alcohol use, treatment foster care as an intervention with serious delinquents, and multi-systemic approaches to working with children with serious mental health problems. The lists do not give a local community much choice for programs that fit their particular needs.

The second problem with the "list" approach involves assuring the fidelity of the approach. Scientifically tested approaches deemed as evidence-based will only yield positive outcomes if they are implemented in the field exactly as they were implemented in the scientific test. This is not always, and in fact it is rarely, possible. Consequently, many approaches that are listed as evidence-based in the literature do not yield the same positive results for the resource strapped communities that try to implement them on a shoestring.

We must be very careful to avoid unintended consequences of policies designed to increase accountability through mandated implementation of evidence-based programs. Requiring too much evidence, too fast, will undoubtedly reduce the support to children and families rather than enhance it. Regulating the use of evidence based principles of effectiveness, common across programs, activities and strategies, provides more local implementation flexibility and will ultimately result in more sustainable efforts. Some of the best results come from activities and strategies that are not necessarily programs.

This better approach might be to use the sixteen prevention principles derived from effective drug abuse prevention research as outlined in NIDA's Preventing Drug Use Among Children and Adolescents published in Oct. 2003. (The list is attached.)

If the SDFSC Advisory Committee established in the "No Child Left Behind" Act was constituted, many of these concerns could be resolved in a timely manner. This Advisory Committee would also be very valuable in helping education be a key player in the community prevention strategies that SAMHSA/CSAP will be calling for in their new Strategic Prevention Framework grant program.

This Advisory Committee could also be instrumental in developing an agreed upon outcome framework for the whole child and a plan for getting there. The framework would be applied at all levels - federal, state and local - and would drive programming and funding.

There are three major targets of prevention that are most effective: parents, schools and communities/environments.

What is known from research is that each domain needs to be reinforced by the other two components to show the greatest impact. Consequently, it will never be enough to put the responsibility solely on the parent, the child, the school or the community.

Within each area there should be universal, selected and targeted programs so everyone gets the prevention message best suited to the circumstances. There needs to be a blend of individual focused and environmental focused efforts.

We have found that multiple strategies in multiple sectors are most effective. It is always a case of more being better than less. Universal primary prevention must not be forgotten in our rush to intervene with children from at risk environments. To do so is likely to increase the numbers of users.

Generally speaking, these are some of the important aspects in the three domains that help raise alcohol and drug free children to adulthood.

The style of parenting employed from infancy makes a tremendous difference. Research has found that the authoritative parent who is not too strict or too lenient, but provides a combination of warmth and structure, is most effective in raising children who are responsible, caring and alcohol and drug free. Children, who believe their parents think drug use is very wrong and would be very upset, use less. Likewise, the more often children and parents eat dinner as a family, the less often teens are involved in tobacco, alcohol or drug use. Researchers are continually learning more about how protective factors such as these build strengths in children.

The seeds of behavior and decision-making are sown long before the child enters kindergarten. Sometimes even in the womb. It is now believed that one in every one hundred live births is affected by exposure to alcohol. Making healthy life choices starts early. The average age of first use is now around 12 years old. We need to focus on raising this age of first use because the adolescent brain goes through many developmental changes. Alcohol and other drug use during this time period can permanently alter the brain's structure leading to less than optimal growth and development. Early alcohol use reduces potential.

In understanding the role and influence of parents, it is important to remember that although parents have a primary responsibility for their children, families do not live in a vacuum. Our homes are not bunkers from reality. Parental guidance is constantly challenged by external influences. We cannot expect parents to be the gatekeeper for their children 24 hours a day for 21 years.

They need help from other parts of society and its institutions. Many of those institutions are not supportive of the role of parents. Even very young children hear or see on a daily basis in popular music, TV, motion pictures, toys, and advertising the not so subtle messages that it's perfectly normal for kids to want to live in their "own" society without the influence of parents. Other messages make children think that they are expected to drink and there is nothing to prevent them from doing so.

Research shows that adolescent alcohol and drug use is inversely related to their perceptions of harm and social disapproval. The greater the negative perceptions, the lower the use.

Research also shows children form expectancies about alcohol on average before age 9 - some before age five.

Most of these messages come from those whose bottom line is profits, not those interested in raising responsible capable human beings. Therefore, to be most effective in preventing alcohol use by teenagers, we must begin to educate children as early as kindergarten.

That is why schools are a critically important component of a community-wide effort and why it is important that each district has funding that makes them a part of community decisions. That is why requiring them to consult with parents and conduct periodic community assessments is critical.

Schools need to be an integral component in all-comprehensive, community-based efforts to reduce childhood and adolescent drinking. In many communities, it's the drug free school coordinator who is the most knowledgeable person about effective prevention strategies but in many districts the coordinator is not a full time position.

An Ohio-based survey in 1997 of Safe and Drug Free School (SDFS) coordinators found that only 11% of the 700 surveyed were employed full time; the remaining had other key positions (assistant principal, teacher, school nurse) in addition to their designation as a SDFS coordinator. Among the part-time coordinators, the number of hours devoted to SDFS work per week ranged from under 10 to 30 hours with approximately 60% providing less than 10 hours per week. A team of people who were trained to assist school staff in meeting the health, behavioral, social and emotional needs of children based on student and employee assistance models would be more effective.

School based programs need to be included at multiple grade levels and delivered in a variety of formats but should follow universal principles of effectiveness as outlined by NIDA.

Evaluation shows that effective school based programs must be theory-based, research-tested, and sustained over time. They include skills training, normative education, and developmentally appropriate information. They use interactive and engaging formats and provide teacher training. However, such programs alone can account for only modest delays or reductions in alcohol use.

We also know from data that the more connected students feel to their school, the less likely they are to engage in potentially destructive behaviors such as alcohol and other drug use. Using this information, school districts are putting more and more effort into social and emotional learning. It has been shown to increase mastery of subject material and motivation to learn; to reduce anxiety; enhance attention and improve study skills; and to increase commitment to school and the time devoted to schoolwork.

Ohio's State Board of Education is working on a set of standards to facilitate safe and supportive learning environments in all Ohio schools. These standards address safety, family involvement, and community partnerships that ensure student assistance programs and administrative procedures. They find it key to train current and future school personnel in this new body of research.

Overall, schools are making great progress in implementing programs based on the six principles of effectiveness for Safe Drug Free Schools and Communities (SDFSC) funding as outlined in the "No Child Left Behind" (NCLB) legislation. (The 6 principles are attached.)

It takes up to two years for money appropriated by Congress to reach the school districts and even longer for implementation of major changes in die language of the Safe and Drug Free Schools and Communities Act. So achievement at this time can only be measured by changes within a state's infrastructure that support quality local programming. Evidence of positive changes in infrastructure based on NCLB, in Ohio include: existence of a plan for enhanced local accountability; available and accessible training and technical assistance related to school improvement; the development of state school operating standards; and integration of programming that addresses the whole child - academic needs as well as social and emotional needs.

In much the same way that family based interventions seek to create a nurturing, supportive family environment, school- and community-based prevention programs expand that supportive network into the larger context.

The greatest efficacy has been observed with programs that include multiple components - family, school, and community. So I would like to mention a few prevention principles useful to communities.

In its Report on Underage Drinking, the Institute of Medicine/National Academies of Science recommended expanding the use of community based interventions. Effective environmental controls that target underage drinking include: reducing commercial and social alcohol availability to youth; establishing and enforcing sanctions for violation of minimum legal drinking age laws and for alcohol misuse, such as drunk driving; and publicizing sanctions and their enforcement. These approaches have direct effects on older teens. Their effects on younger kids are indirect by reducing the amount of alcohol in the youth 'social pipeline', so that older teens will be less likely to provide alcohol to younger ones. In addition, the report calls for restrictions on advertising messages seen by youth. These approaches also have an effect on drug use because most young people use alcohol before they move on to other drugs.

Finally, research has shown that people are often most attentive to a message when a personal experience causes them to sit up and take notice. Referred to as teachable moments, these events often provide a window of opportunity to deliver information that under other circumstances might be ignored. An NIAAA supported study of adolescents entering the emergency room, indicated the importance of capitalizing on such a teachable moment.

Adolescents entering the ER following an alcohol-related event received a brief intervention on alcohol. Follow-up assessments showed that patients who received the motivational intervention had a significantly lower incidence of drinking and driving, traffic violations, alcohol-related injuries, and alcohol-related problems than patients who received standard care. Both conditions showed reduced alcohol consumption, however the group receiving the intervention had greater reductions in negative consequences.

On December 19, 2003, DHHS released the latest data from Monitoring the Future. The Director of ONDCP, John Walters joined Secretary Tommy Thompson in commenting on the 11% reduction in adolescent use that the national data showed. His words are revealing and important to keep in mind if our Nation hopes to reduce and prevent youth alcohol use. “This survey shows that when we push back against the drug problem, it gets smaller.

Fewer teens are using drugs because of the deliberate and serious messages they have received about the dangers of drugs from their parents, leaders, and prevention efforts like our National Youth Anti-Drug Media Campaign.

Having fewer youth use drugs is important because we know that if young people can abstain from drugs before they graduate from high school, they are much less likely to use and have problems with them later.” They are also more likely to graduate from college and not need publicly funded treatment.

This National survey shows that what we are doing is currently having an impact. The numbers are moving in the right direction. The biggest and most cost-effective movement in the numbers comes from prevention. Prevention is most effective when parents, schools and communities work together and larger entities such as government, media and corporations are supportive.

Schools could play a more important role if they:

1. based their programs, activities and strategies on evidence based prevention principles and the 6 principles of effectiveness in NCLB;

2. had the funding to hire full time drug free school coordinators for each district who would head up teams of trained personnel and reach out to parents and the community as a whole;
3. had confidence all districts would have continual SDFSC funding under the same guidelines for a sustained period of time;
4. had the benefits of better federal level coordination and faster dissemination of new research findings that would come with a constituted Federal SDFSC Advisory Committee; and
5. had the benefit of knowledge gained from more federally funded research focusing on what motivates children to drink, the extent of second hand effects of alcohol, the relationship of alcohol in every unnatural death, and effective prevention efforts especially for children aged 9 to 15, all of which NIAAA is willing to undertake.

Thank you very much for being interested enough in the success of children to make sure that schools have the tools necessary to keep children alcohol and other drug free.

I would be very happy to answer any questions you might have.

Hope Taft

PREVENTING DRUG USE AMONG CHILDREN AND ADOLESCENTS

16 prevention principles from the National Institute on Drug Abuse (N1DA) of the U.S. Department of Health and Human Services, that reflects the latest research. (2003)

Principle l

Prevention programs should enhance protective factors and reverse or reduce risk factors. The potential impact of risk and protective factors changes with age. For example, risk factors with the family have a greater impact on the younger child, while association with drug-abusing peers may be a more significant risk factor for an adolescent. Early intervention with risk factors often has a greater impact that later intervention by changing a child's life path away from problems and toward more positive behavior.

Principle 2

Prevention programs should address all forms of drug abuse, including underage use of legal drugs; the use of illegal drugs; and the inappropriate use of legally obtained substances, prescription medications, or over-the-counter drugs.

Principle 3

Prevention programs should address the type of drug abuse problem in the local community, target modifiable risk factors, and strengthen identified protective factors.

Principle 4

Prevention programs should be tailored to address risks specific to population or audience characteristics to improve program effectiveness.

Principle 5

Family-based prevention programs should enhance family bonding and relationships and include parenting skills, practice in enforcing family policies on substance use, and training in drug education and information.

Principle 6

Prevention programs can be designed to intervene as early as preschool to address risk factors for drug abuse.

Principle 7

Prevention programs for elementary school children should target improving academic and social-emotional learning to address risk factors for drug abuse, such as early aggression, academic failure, and school dropout. Education should focus on self-control, emotional awareness, communication, social problem-solving, and academic support, especially in reading.

Principle 8

Prevention programs for middle or junior high and high school students should increase academic and social competence with the following skills: study habits and academic support; communication, peer relationships, self-efficacy and assertiveness; drug resistance skills, reinforcement of anti-drug attitudes and strengthening of personal commitments against drug abuse.

Principle 9

Prevention programs aimed at general populations at key transition points can produce beneficial effects even among high-risk families and children. Such interventions do not single out risk populations and, therefore, reduce labeling.

Principle 10

Community prevention programs that combine two or more effective programs can be more effective than a single program alone.

Principle 11

Community prevention programs reaching populations in multiple settings are most effective when they present consistent, community-wide messages in each setting.

Principle 12

When communities adapt programs to match their needs, community norms, or differing cultural requirements, they should retain the core elements of the original research-based intervention.

Principle 13

Prevention programs should be long-term with repeated interventions to reinforce the original prevention goals.

Principle 14

Prevention programs should include teacher training on good classroom management practices.

Principle 15

Prevention programs are most effective when they employ interactive techniques that allow for active involvement in learning about drug abuse and reinforcing skills.

Principle 16

Research-based prevention programs can be cost-effective.

Principles of Effectiveness, SDFSC Program in NCLB

The No Child Left Behind Act specifies that any program or activity funded through the SDFSC program must meet the following "Principles of Effectiveness".

1. Be based upon an assessment of objective data about community needs for the activities;
2. Be based upon performance measures established by the LEA;
3. Be based upon "scientifically based research" that the program or activity will be effective (there is a waiver for innovative programs with a likelihood of success);
4. Be periodically evaluated with the results used to improve the program or activity;
5. Be based on as analysis of risk factors and protective factors; and
6. Include consultation with parents

INDEX

A

B

C

D

E

F

G

H

I

L

M

N

O

P

R

T

U

V

W

Y

Z